NOODLES
the new way

sri owen

photographs by Gus Filgate

Introduction 4

Noodle basics 8

Vegetarian noodles 48

Noodles with seafood 68

Noodles with poultry 86

Noodles with meat 104

Noodle salads 122

Glossary 140

Acknowledgements and Bibliography 143

Index 144

CONTENTS

*for Roger, Irwan and Daniel,
my most outspoken critics –
but they all love noodles*

Throughout the recipes in this book both metric and imperial
quantities are given. Use either all metric or all imperial, as
the two are not necessarily interchangeable.

The basic concept of noodles is so brilliant, yet so obvious, that I have never believed the story about Marco Polo teaching the Emperor of China how to make spaghetti, and then returning to Italy to show the Italians how to make noodles. I'm sure noodles and spaghetti have both been invented in different places several times over, and every time it happens there is public rejoicing.

INTRODUCTION

Considering the passion I've always had for rice, why am I writing a book about noodles? There are plenty of reasons – and I still love rice as much as ever.

Provided you've got all the ingredients ready prepared, you can cook a one-dish gourmet meal based on noodles in less than 10 minutes. You won't find any other staple food that lets you do that and offers such a variety of accompaniments to choose from – an infinite variety, in fact, because you can go on improvising for ever. Noodles, like other kinds of pasta, are mostly starch, and will absorb and set off the flavour of any sauce, or whatever else they're cooked and served with.

Noodles have another attraction for me: they are not snobs, they are at ease in any company and are perhaps the most democratic of foods. There are no right and wrong ways to eat them, just as there are no right or wrong times. They fit in anywhere. No one will mind whether you eat them elegantly, twirling them round a fork and never spilling a drop of sauce, or shovel them up with spoon or chopsticks and end up with one long one hanging down your chin, like the tail of a mouse being swallowed by an owl. Follow the example of Asian noodle-slurpers – tuck a few strands into your mouth with whatever tools are to hand, then suck them in powerfully, relying on the uprush of noodle to bring with it all the sauce and cut-up fragments of meat and veg, steaming-hot.

If someone asks, 'Why don't noodles come from the factory already chopped into convenient lengths?', the answer is because then they wouldn't be so much fun to eat and therefore wouldn't taste as good. Alternatively, give the Chinese answer – because long noodles are a symbol of long life, and cutting them short, whether in the factory, in the kitchen or at the table, might seem to suggest that long life is something we don't care about.

Cooking noodles is also very simple and almost as easy as eating them. However, a beginner can benefit from a little help and experience, and an expert remains expert by continually learning. Like any work of art, a great noodle dish needs knowledge and

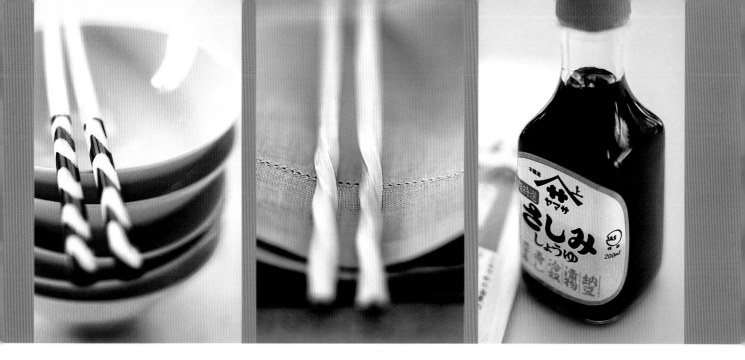

forethought, however rapid the actual cooking may be. Your aim is to make something that combines contrasting flavours and textures in perfect harmony. The noodles themselves are, if you like, the canvas on which the picture is painted.

A Chinese or Japanese cook would say that you must keep in mind the principles of yin and yang, and remember that some foods are 'hot', others 'cold'. Someone from Southeast Asia would emphasize the balance of textures (we usually say that there should be at least two, possibly three – crunchy, chewy and soft – in a perfectly composed dish) and flavours (at least two out of the basic five – sweet, salty, hot, sour or bitter, and aromatic).

Remember that excellent Japanese film *Tampopo*, about the woman with the noodle bar who was determined to make perfect noodles, and was helped in this by the comments of her highly critical customers. As I watched the film, I had the impression I could almost feel and taste every mouthful – I certainly came out hungrier than I went in.

Japanese cooks are perhaps lucky in having traditional models of what perfect noodles (and perfect anything else) ought to be. When I was younger I too paid great attention to cooking my own country's food exactly as I remembered it from my childhood in Sumatra and Java. Probably this is a useful part of anyone's training; you learn the rules and

practise them until they are second nature. Then you start to bend and break them and make something new.

In the thirty-odd years that I have lived in London, Asian ingredients, flavours and techniques have poured into restaurants, high-street shops and everyone's kitchens at home. It has been an exhilarating process to watch and take part in, a liberation of European taste-buds – at least for those who have not become enslaved to industrial fast food. These new resources create the need for new knowledge, the knowledge of how to use them. That is why I have devoted the past twenty years or so to writing about food – Asian food in particular – and teaching people to cook. I want my readers and my students to share my love of food, and also to understand how and why Asians cook as they do.

However, I no longer only want to re-create what is perfect or authentic from the past. The best food stores, market stalls and supermarkets now bring us such a choice of fresh produce from so many countries that the imaginative cook may well feel like an artist who has been given a paint-box full of completely new colours. All we have to do is to work out the best ways to use them.

In this book, I describe and explain the basic techniques, the rules of noodle cookery. Then I show how tastes and textures from different sources can work together to make something really delicious. It's not always necessary to prepare everything from scratch; you can buy ready-prepared and ready-cooked ingredients that will cut cooking time, and I also give recipes and suggestions for making your own stocks, sauces, dressings and pastes, so that you needn't have any left-over herbs to go bad or spices to go dry and lose their flavour. Your fridge and freezer will keep you supplied with home-made mixes ready for instant use in just the quantities you need.

By the time you have cooked your way through the recipes that follow, you will have a thorough grounding in noodle cookery and a good basic knowledge of how ingredients are used together. If you like to 'cook by the book' and take no chances, you will have a new repertoire of dishes that will go down well at all sorts of occasions and in any company. If, however, you want to strike out on your own, be a brilliant improviser at short notice or spend an hour pondering the precise balance of smooth and crisp, sour and salt in something very simple but quite outrageous – then I hope you will find some help here as well as encouragement.

Above all, remember that noodles are not just fast food, but tasty and nutritious food as well.

Main picture: fine dried egg noodles;
1 Asian dried egg noodles;
2 fresh oily noodles;
3 dried egg noodles in blocks.

NOODLE BASICS

First, a catalogue of noodle types, arranged by the raw materials from which they are made.

Wheat flour: Chinese wheat-flour noodles (including flavoured noodles and egg noodles); Japanese udon, *kishimen*, *hiyamugi* and somen; ramen; Chinese wonton skins (round and square); spring roll (*lumpia*) wrappers

Rice flour: Round and flat noodles of all sizes; rice vermicelli, rice sticks; rice paper wrappers (Vietnamese *banh trang*), round and triangular

Mung-bean flour: Cellophane noodles

Buckwheat flour: Korean buckwheat noodles (*naengmyon*), Japanese soba and cha-soba

From these, we can choose just four basic types which will be sufficient for most recipes in this book. These are the most popular and the most widely available – either in supermarkets or in ethnic food shops. It is advisable to buy dry noodles, imported from the country where that particular type of noodle originated, as they will have a much better flavour and texture.

The basic types of noodle

As a general rule, if you are cooking for more than 4 people, or creating your own dish, allow the following quantities per person of uncooked noodles: for a first course 60 g / 2 oz; for a main course or one-bowl meal 85–115 g / 3–4 oz.

Cellophane noodles are exceptions, as they are more often used as a stuffing or a garnish than as a staple. For these, follow the exact quantities shown in the recipe.

Many shops sell noodles already shaped as the basis of stylish food presentations – 'nests' are especially popular. I would not recommend buying these as, when you precook them, you will have to shake them loose, with the result that they lose their shapes. If you don't do this, the noodle strands will stick together and cook unevenly. Nests and baskets are fine if you want partly raw containers for your food, but I would not advise you to eat them.

EGG NOODLES – ROUND AND FLAT:

These are available in several grades, from very fine to quite coarse and thick. Their country of origin is China, and they are widely exported, so buy packets of dried noodles manufactured in China.

❹ fresh flat Asian egg noodles;
❺ supermarket fresh egg noodles;
❻ supermarket dried egg noodles;
❼ fresh fine Asian noodles.

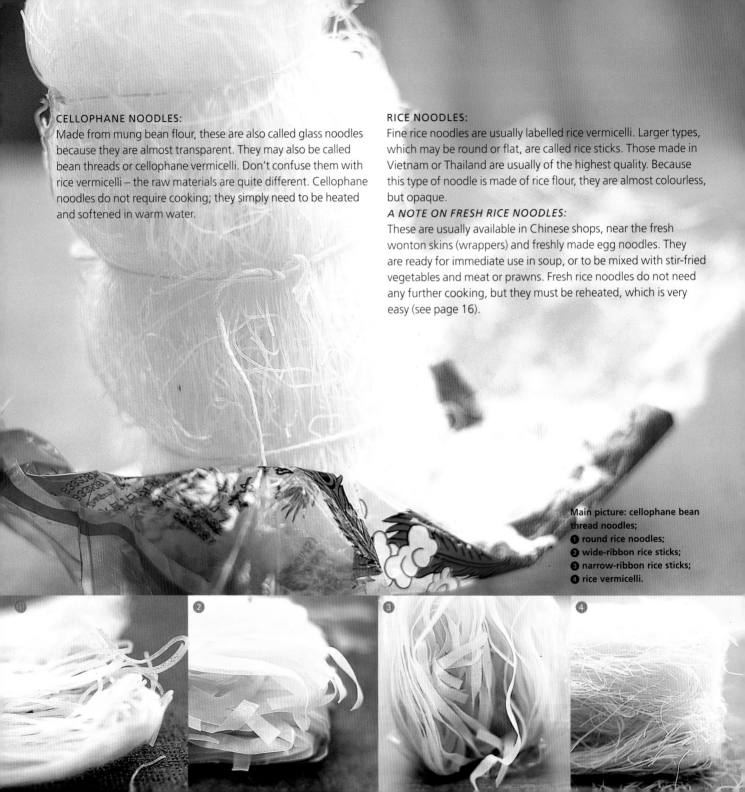

CELLOPHANE NOODLES:

Made from mung bean flour, these are also called glass noodles because they are almost transparent. They may also be called bean threads or cellophane vermicelli. Don't confuse them with rice vermicelli – the raw materials are quite different. Cellophane noodles do not require cooking; they simply need to be heated and softened in warm water.

RICE NOODLES:

Fine rice noodles are usually labelled rice vermicelli. Larger types, which may be round or flat, are called rice sticks. Those made in Vietnam or Thailand are usually of the highest quality. Because this type of noodle is made of rice flour, they are almost colourless, but opaque.

A NOTE ON FRESH RICE NOODLES:

These are usually available in Chinese shops, near the fresh wonton skins (wrappers) and freshly made egg noodles. They are ready for immediate use in soup, or to be mixed with stir-fried vegetables and meat or prawns. Fresh rice noodles do not need any further cooking, but they must be reheated, which is very easy (see page 16).

Main picture: cellophane bean thread noodles;
❶ round rice noodles;
❷ wide-ribbon rice sticks;
❸ narrow-ribbon rice sticks;
❹ rice vermicelli.

JAPANESE NOODLES:
These are further subdivided into three types:
Soba noodles, which are made with 80–90 per cent buckwheat flour (the rest is wheat flour), giving them a slightly brownish colour. Buckwheat flour by itself would make the noodles too brittle. Look for them, neatly cut into sticks about 20 cm / 8 inches long, packed in Japan, and labelled entirely in Japanese. If the label is entirely or partly in English, the contents have probably not been made for the Japanese market. In that case, they may not be of the highest standard, and they may contain a higher proportion of wheat flour.

Udon, which are usually fat round noodles, white in colour and made of wheat flour and water. Flat udon are sometimes found.
Somen, which are fine white noodles made of wheat flour and water, with a little oil. Packed in neat bundles (if they are imported from Japan, they are often tied with colourful ribbons), they are available from most Japanese shops, but rarely from elsewhere. Like soba, they are often served cold with a dipping sauce.

Main picture: soba noodles;
❺ reconstituted udon noodles;
❻ round udon noodles;
❼ flat udon noodles;
❽ somen noodles.

Main picture: triangular
rice paper;
❶ round wonton skins;
❷ square wonton skins;
❸ spring roll wrappers.

The basic types of wrapper

Four types of wrapper will be enough to fit the needs of the recipes featured in this book. These wrappers are the most popular and the most widely available – either in supermarkets or in ethnic food shops.

RICE PAPERS (VIETNAMESE *BANH TRANG*):
These are not the rolled sheets of edible paper that such things as macaroons are baked on. They are stiff and very brittle (so they need careful handling). They are sold dry, usually in clear plastic packets, and come in several sizes but only in two shapes – discs and triangles. The discs, which are the ones I most often use, can be bought in at least three sizes: small (15 cm / 6 inches diameter), medium (21 cm / 8½ inches) and large (29 cm / 11½ inches).

Before use, rice papers must be softened. Immerse them, one sheet at a time, in a bowl of warm water. In less than a minute, they become soft and pliable. Lift the sheet out carefully – it will now tear easily – and lay it out flat on a tray. Dab away the excess water with kitchen paper, then arrange the filling or stuffing on top of it, and roll it up (see the recipe for Vietnamese Rice Paper Rolls with Herb Salad on page 130.)

Filled rolls can be deep-fried or steamed. Be careful not to make any tear in the rice paper if it is to be fried. Even a small hole will let the oil get inside. If rice papers are used as wrappers for food that has already been cooked, or for fresh raw vegetables and salad leaves, then the papers themselves must be softened in hot (but not boiling) water. This will not only soften the paper but heat it sufficiently to cook it.

SPRING ROLL WRAPPERS:
These are usually available from the freezers in Chinese and many other Asian shops. They come in three sizes of square: 12 cm / 5 inches; 24 cm / 10 inches; and 30 cm / 12 inches. The pastry dries out very quickly if it gets a chance. The best way to work with it is to thaw a whole packet, then carefully peel the sheets off one by one. The ones you don't use can be re-frozen. Once the sheets have been separated, they stay separate and you can fill and roll them quickly, even after they have been re-frozen.

WONTON SKINS:
You can buy these fresh or frozen, usually in packs of 175–225 g / 6–8 oz, or in larger packs about twice this weight. They are very thin pastry squares, about 7.5 cm / 3 inches on a side. You can also get round ones, about the same diameter. Both shapes can be bought either thin, for frying, or slightly thicker, for steaming. Being made with eggs, wonton skins (of whatever shape) don't stick to each other.

how to cook the basic types of noodle

There are essentially just two or three simple stages in the cooking of most types of noodle, all of them quite short and simple – precooking (usually followed by refreshing) and reheating or further cooking.

For perfect results (tender but still firm), noodles must first be precooked for the right length of time, then refreshed under cold running water – to stop further cooking – until cold. They are then reheated or cooked further, as required. Cooking can, if required, be done some time before the noodles are to be eaten, but preferably not more than one hour ahead.

Some types of noodle, if left in a colander more than half an hour, will cling together and form a solid lump. Others, especially better-quality noodles, can be refreshed and left to drain for up to an hour, yet still remain separate.

If you want to shape or arrange your noodles, or make them lie straight on the plate or fold them over, the time to do this is immediately after precooking. As long as you are reasonably careful when you reheat them, they will keep the shape you gave them. In this way you can style them for a smart presentation, arranged to suit your other ingredients.

Precooking noodles

EGG NOODLES:
Half-fill a large saucepan with water and bring to the boil. Add 1 teaspoon of salt and adjust the heat to keep the water at a rolling boil. Add the noodles and use long bamboo chopsticks or a fork to move the noodles about so that the bundles loosen and separate somewhat. Cook for 2½–3 minutes.

Transfer the noodles to a colander and hold them under cold running water, agitating them gently with your fingers so that they stay separate and the whole mass cools quickly and completely. Leave them in the colander to drain.

RICE NOODLES:
Rice sticks, or wide ribbon-type rice noodles, should be cooked, then refreshed under cold running water as egg noodles. Fine rice noodles or rice vermicelli need only be soaked in a pan or bowl of hot but not boiling water. Make sure the noodles are completely immersed, cover and leave for 6–8 minutes. Drain them, put them under cold running water for 2 minutes and drain again.

SOBA NOODLES, UDON, SOMEN:
Cook these as you would egg noodles but without salt. Soba and somen should be boiled for 2–2½ minutes only; udon for 3–3½ minutes. (If you cook Japanese noodles the Japanese way as below, which involves adding cold water three times during cooking, the whole process will take up to 5 minutes.) Refresh under cold running water as described above.

CELLOPHANE NOODLES OR CELLOPHANE VERMICELLI:
Put the noodles in a large bowl and cover them completely with hot water – this should be hot water from a kettle that has boiled and then been left to stand for 5 minutes. Leave the noodles under the hot water for 5–8 minutes. Drain them, refresh under cold running water and drain them again.

THE JAPANESE WAY:
For soba and fine egg noodles, as well as for somen (the fine Japanese wheat-flour noodles), the Japanese cooking technique ensures the noodles do not become too soft through overcooking. Half-fill a pan with cold water and bring to the boil. Add the noodles, leave them in the boiling water for 1 minute, then add a cup (225 ml / 8 fl oz) of cold water. Bring the water back to the boil and boil gently for 1 more minute. Then add a second cup of cold water. Repeat this cycle once more: 1 minute boiling, then a third cup of cold water. Taste a short piece of noodle. It should be still firm, but taste cooked. I have found that noodles cooked this way require a total cooking time of 5 minutes. Drain, and refresh under cold running water. There is usually no need to add any salt at this stage.

Refreshing precooked noodles under cold running water until they are quite cold stops further cooking and reduces the chances of them sticking together.

Reheating noodles

Noodles cooked as described on the previous pages need to be reheated before serving, unless (as sometimes happens) the recipe instructs you otherwise. The following are the simplest methods of reheating:

If you are preparing and cooking noodles for 2 people only, simply put the precooked noodles into a sieve (a conical one, if you like, but any shape will do) and pour a kettleful of boiling water over the noodles in a steady stream which should last (if possible) up to 30 seconds. This will loosen the bundle of cold precooked noodles, heating them at the same time. Give the sieve a good shake to drain off all the water. Then arrange the noodles on plates or in bowls, or stir-fry them further, according to the recipe.

If you are cooking noodles for 4 people or more, the easiest way to reheat them is in a large saucepan of boiling water. The water should be actually boiling when you plunge into it the sieve containing the noodles. Keep the noodles submerged for 20 seconds, no more. Then lift them out, give the sieve a shake to drain them well, and continue as per the recipe.

Storing uncooked and cooked noodles

Fresh noodles should, obviously, be cooked and eaten as soon as possible, but what about packets of dried noodles? Once you have opened the packet, should you cook the whole lot or can you keep some of them uncooked for a few days or weeks? This really depends on how the noodles were packed. Straight noodles, that are easily separated, can be kept in a zip-lock bag or a glass jar for weeks or even months. Noodles that are packed in a skein or a tangled mass are usually impossible to separate neatly, and once the packet is opened they should all be cooked together.

Cooked noodles should, ideally, be eaten as fresh as possible. If you have cooked far more than people can eat, however, the leftovers will keep perfectly well in a covered bowl in the fridge for at least a week, and can be reheated and served again in almost any of the dishes described in this book.

I would not, of course, serve leftover noodles to my guests, but I'm not sure that they would notice if I did, and I eat them myself with enjoyment.

making noodles at home

It is always a pleasure to make things by hand – up to a point.
The only tools you really need for making fresh noodles are a rolling
pin, a sharp knife and a straight edge. A pasta machine does make
the job quicker, however, and the noodles are perhaps a little more
even in width and thickness.

Wheat flour egg noodles   Serves 4–6

1½ tablespoons salt
1 egg yolk
675 g / 1½ lb plain flour, plus
more for dusting

1 In a bowl, dissolve the salt in 225 ml / 8 fl oz cold water by stirring it with a fork. Add the egg yolk and beat the mixture until everything is well blended.

2 Sift the flour on a work surface or into a large bowl and make a well in the centre. Pour in the water and egg mixture, a little at a time. As you pour, mix the flour and the liquid gently with the other hand to make a dough (you may not need all the egg mix).

3 Then, with both hands, knead the dough vigorously until it is smooth and firm. Use the heel of one hand to push the dough firmly across the work surface, then roll it up and work it with both hands to get rid of creases and air bubbles. This kneading will take about 8 minutes.

4 Put the dough into a bowl and cover with a damp tea-towel. Leave in a cool place (not in the fridge) for 2–3 hours.

5 On a floured work surface, roll one-quarter of the dough to make a thin, more or less rectangular, sheet. This rolling will take some time and effort – the dough by now has become quite elastic.

6 Once the dough is rolled out thin and even, leave it for 30 seconds or so to dry out slightly, then sprinkle a little flour over it. Fold the sheet to make 3 equal layers. Then, at right angles to the folds, cut the dough into strips, using a ruler as a guide. The width of the strips may vary from very narrow to 1 cm / ½ inch or even 2.5 cm / 1 inch wide, according to your preference and how you intend to cook the noodles. Repeat this process until all the dough has been rolled, folded and cut up.

7 Spread the noodles out on a large tray and leave them to dry for 5–10 minutes. Then cook them in plenty of boiling water, as described in How to cook the basic types of noodle on page 14.

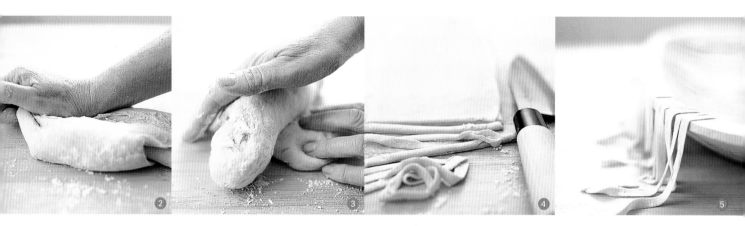

Making wheat flour egg noodles: ❶ Mix the flour and egg mixture gently to make a dough. ❷ Using the heel of the hand, knead the dough firmly across the work surface until the dough is smooth and firm. ❸ Roll the dough up and work with both hands to eliminate creases and air bubbles. ❹ After resting, rolling and brief drying, fold the dough into three and cut across into strips. ❺ Spread the noodles out to dry.

Soba (buckwheat) noodles

If you have a pasta machine and a little experience of making pasta, you will have no difficulty in making soba. Even if you don't have a machine, you can roll out, fold and cut the dough as described for wheat-flour egg noodles opposite. You do, however, need to use Japanese buckwheat flour. Serves 4–6

1 large egg
355 g / 12½ oz Japanese buckwheat flour
155 g / 5½ oz plain flour, plus more for dusting

❶ Whisk the egg in a bowl, add 210 ml / 7½ fl oz cold water and whisk again.
❷ Combine the two flours in a bowl. Sift them into another bowl, then put the sifted flour into a food processor. With the machine running, slowly pour just enough of the egg and water mixture into the flour to form a dough.
❸ Transfer this dough to a bowl and knead it for a minute or so. Divide the dough into 6 pieces, roll each piece into a small ball, and leave these to rest under an upturned bowl for about 30 minutes.
❹ Put a ball of dough into a pasta machine and roll it to make a thin sheet. Repeat this process until you have 6 sheets of dough. Then put each sheet into the cutter. Hang the cut noodles to dry for a few minutes, just as you would if you were making pasta. Then cook them as described on page 14.

basic stocks

As in most cuisines, good stocks form the basis of a wide range of soups and sauces. Ready-made fresh stocks are increasingly available, but nothing can beat the flavour of a homemade stock — and they are so cheap to make.

Dashi

This Japanese stock made from dried bonito (tuna flakes) forms the basis for most Japanese soups. Japanese food shops sell instant dashi, which is good but not as good as the fresh homemade product. Once you have found your kelp (*konbu*) and dried bonito flakes (*katsuobushi*), the rest is easy. **Makes about 1.1 litre / 2 pints**

1 piece of kelp, about 5 cm / 2 inches long
4 tablespoons bonito flakes

❶ Put the kelp into a saucepan with about 1 litre / 1¾ pints of water. Bring the water almost to the boil.

❷ Take out the kelp, bring the water to the boil, and add 115 ml / 4 fl oz of cold water and the bonito flakes.

❸ Bring the water back to the boil, then immediately take the pan off the heat. Let it stand for 30 seconds. Then strain the stock through a sieve lined with muslin.

❹ Use the stock as directed in recipes. It can be stored, in a covered bowl, in the fridge for up to a week.

Basic fish stock

Use any white fish heads, bones and trimmings, with the addition of one small whole fish – a plaice, for example. For a stronger stock, near the end of cooking add about 250 g / 9 oz of well-washed prawn shells. **Makes about 1.1 litres / 2 pints**

about 900 g / 2 lb head, bones and trimmings of white fish
1 small whole fish, such as plaice
1 onion, sliced
1 celery stalk, coarsely chopped
½ teaspoon salt
250 g / 9 oz prawn shells (optional)

❶ Put all the ingredients, except the prawn shells if using them, in a large saucepan with 1.4–1.75 litres / 2½–3 pints cold water. Bring to the boil and simmer gently for 20–25 minutes.

❷ If you are using prawn shells, add them now, with an additional 115 ml / 4 fl oz water. Bring the stock back to the boil and simmer for another 10 minutes.

❸ Strain the stock and leave it to cool. Store in the fridge for 3–4 days, until needed.

Plainly cooked egg noodles in a tasty and nourishing vegetable stock (see recipe overleaf), make a simple but satisfying soup.

Basic miso stock

This can be used as a base for many different noodle soups. It is important that the stock should be perfectly clear and not have too many contrasting flavours. Therefore, the other ingredients of the noodle soup must not overpower the stock, and vice versa. Each ingredient should retain its own flavour, distinct from the others but not drowning them. **Makes about 1.75 litres / 3 pints**

1 shallot, chopped
1 garlic clove, chopped
1-cm / ½-inch slice of root ginger
2 tablespoons rice (or barley) and soybean miso (page 141)

❶ Put all the ingredients in a large saucepan with 2 litres / 3½ pints cold water. Bring to the boil and simmer, uncovered, for 1–2 hours.
❷ Strain the stock through a sieve lined with muslin or kitchen paper. Be patient – it will take a long time for the stock to strain through.
❸ Cover the bowl. The stock can now be stored in the fridge and will stay fresh for 7–10 days. Use as directed in your chosen recipe.

Basic Asian stock

This is how basic non-meat stock is made for Thai cooking. If you wish, you can add some vegetables to make a basic vegetable stock. The quantities of water and salt are the same whether or not you add extra vegetables. If you do add vegetables, you will need to let the stock simmer for a total of 40–50 minutes.
Makes 1.75 litres / 3 pints

3 shallots, coarsely chopped
1 lemon grass stalk, cut across into three
2.5-cm / 1-inch piece of galangal (page 140), sliced
1 large red chilli, deseeded and split lengthwise into 2 pieces (optional)
½ teaspoon salt

❶ Put all the ingredients into a large saucepan with 1.75 litres / 3 pints cold water. Bring to the boil and simmer gently for 20–25 minutes, skimming from time to time.
❷ Strain the stock into a bowl and leave to cool. Discard the solids. Store in the fridge (for up to 10 days) until needed.
Variation for basic vegetable stock: Add other vegetables, such as carrots, celery or a potato or two, to this Thai stock and it becomes a basic vegetable stock that can be used in recipes with no connection whatever with Thailand. The only preparation such vegetables require is cutting into quite large chunks. Just put them in the pan with the other ingredients and simmer for an additional 20–25 minutes – that is, 40–50 minutes altogether. Then strain the stock and store as described above.

Basic chicken stock

For best results, use the whole chicken – a free-range bird if possible. Cut it lengthwise into halves and wash the inside cavity very thoroughly. Discard any remains that may be clinging to the bones, otherwise the stock may taste bitter.
Makes about 2 litres / 3½ pints

1 whole chicken, preferably free-range
1 large onion, cut into quarters (the onion
skin can go in as well, if you like)
1 teaspoon salt

1 With a sharp knife, cut the two pieces of breast meat from the breast bone. Put the two halves of the carcass and the two pieces of breast meat in a large saucepan. Pour in enough cold water to cover the meat and the carcass (about 2.5 litres / 4½ pints). Add the onion and salt and bring the water to the boil. Lower the heat so that the water temperature is just above simmering point. This is important, because at this temperature the froth will rise to the surface and you can skim it off.
2 When the stock has been simmering for 20 minutes, take out the two pieces of breast meat with a slotted spoon, and set them aside. When they are cold they can be sliced very thinly and used in the recipes on pages 72, 87 or 90.

3 The rest of the chicken should be left simmering for a further 2 hours or thereabouts. Add more cold water as required to replace what has evaporated and, of course, you should skim the froth from the surface from time to time.
4 After 2 hours of simmering, take the pan from the heat. Let the stock cool a little, then strain it through a fine-meshed sieve into a large bowl. The carcass should now be thrown away (the meat that is still on it has no flavour and is not worth eating).
5 The stock, when cool, can be stored in the fridge. Next day, skim off and discard the fat that has hardened on the surface. The stock can now be stored in the fridge until needed; it will keep perfectly well for at least 5 days. It can also be frozen in an ice-cube tray, and will keep in the freezer for up to 3 months.

Beef stock

I find the best-tasting beef stock is made with brisket. Makes about 1.5 litres / 2¾ pints

1.4 kg / 3 lb brisket of beef, cut into about 6 pieces
1 teaspoon salt

❶ Put the meat and salt in a large saucepan with 3 litres / 5¼ pints cold water. Bring to the boil, lower the heat and simmer, letting the water just bubble gently, for 1 hour. Skim off the froth from time to time.

❷ After 1 hour, top up the water to its original level, bring it back to the boil, then lower the heat and continue to simmer for a further 2 hours.

❸ Let the stock cool a little and then strain it through a sieve lined with muslin into a large bowl. Refrigerate, then discard the fat that solidifies on the surface of the stock.

❹ Use the stock as required. The pieces of beef can be used in a casserole if you wish, but they have very little flavour left in them.

dipping sauces

I have collected or created several dipping sauces, ranging from the mild Japanese original to some eclectic and spicier ones. When the recipe shows the number it will serve, e.g. 'Serves 4–6', this amount is 'one measure'. A few recipes require more than this. Noodles with a dipping sauce are usually served as a light one-bowl lunch.

Beetroot and anchovy dipping sauce

In another recipe, I commend a lavish seafood hotpot to people who live near the sea and can buy locally caught fish fresh every day. This recipe, by contrast, is for people who grow their own beetroot. It is not necessary to catch your own anchovies.

The method of cooking beetroot here is taken from Christopher Lloyd's *Gardener Cook*. He says the best way to cook beetroot is to put them on a baking tray with the oven set at 150°C/300°F/gas 2 for 1–1½ hours (small beetroot) or 2–3 hours (large ones).

As with other home-made pickles and chutneys, this dip will keep in airtight jars in the fridge for up to a fortnight, possibly a little longer. Like the Spicy Avocado Dipping Sauce (page 30), it can be eaten with cold soba noodles or any other kind of noodles, cold, warm or hot. You can also use it as a dressing for hot egg noodles.

Makes 600 ml / 1 pint

450 g / 1 lb young whole beetroot, cooked as above
115–175 g / 4–6 oz canned anchovies in olive oil, drained and chopped
2 shallots, finely chopped
1 garlic clove, crushed
1 teaspoon finely chopped root ginger
2–6 bird's-eye chillies, deseeded and finely chopped
2 tablespoons finely chopped parsley
3 tablespoons white wine vinegar or Japanese brown rice vinegar
1 tablespoon extra-virgin olive oil
2 teaspoons brown sugar
a little salt or ½ teaspoon fish sauce (*nam pla*, page 140)

❶ The skins of the cooked beetroots can be peeled off with your fingers, under cold running water if you prefer. Dice the peeled beetroot quite small and put in a glass serving bowl.
❷ Mix in all the other ingredients and blend well with a fork. Leave at room temperature for 30 minutes.
❸ Taste and adjust the seasoning. The flavour should be hot, sour and slightly sweet. The dip can be served immediately.
❹ For storage, transfer the dip to a jar with an airtight lid, and keep it in the fridge for up to 14 days.

Japanese dipping sauce

My first encounter with cold noodles took place when I was in Hiroshima in 1991. I had been told that in Japan in July and August the weather is so hot that soba noodles and somen are often served cold or even chilled on ice.

   In a noodle bar next to the railway station, I pointed to a picture of soba noodles beautifully presented in a basket. Accompanying them was a bowl of dipping sauce. The food was served, and I found I did not care for it at all – probably because I wasn't expecting noodles to be cold. Even in tropical Java, we had been brought up on piping-hot noodle soup or fried noodles. However, when a Japanese friend invited me to her home and gave me more cold soba noodles with dipping sauce I enjoyed them very much; so, if they are an acquired taste, at least the taste is acquired quickly. **Makes about 600 ml / 1 pint**

2 tablespoons dried bonito flakes (*katsuobushi*, page 141) or
2 tablespoons dried shrimp
600 ml / 1 pint Dashi (page 21)
150 ml / ¼ pint dark soy sauce
3 tablespoons mirin (page 141)
½ teaspoon sugar

❶ If using bonito flakes, put all the ingredients except the bonito flakes into a saucepan and bring the mixture to the boil. Then add the bonito flakes and take the pan off the heat. Leave the bonito flakes to steep in the liquid for 20–30 seconds. Then strain the sauce and discard the solids.

❷ If using dried shrimp, soak these in boiling water for 5 minutes. Then drain them and discard the soaking water. Put the soaked shrimp into a saucepan and add all the other ingredients. Bring this mixture to the boil and then take it off the heat. Let it cool a little, then strain it and discard the solids.

❸ Let the dipping sauce cool to room temperature before serving. In an airtight jar, it can be stored in the fridge for up to 1 month.

Spicy avocado dipping sauce

Avocado trees grow prolifically in the tropics. There was a large one in my parents' garden, producing enormous quantities of fruit, but we never thought of eating the avocados as a savoury. My mother had learned from Dutch books and from her Dutch friends that they should be made into mousse for dessert. I hated this mousse, because it was always made with canned condensed milk and contained far more sugar than was good for me.

Now, however, Indonesians have realized that avocado with plenty of chillies and lime juice makes an excellent dip for crudités and cooked prawns. In this book, I am introducing it as a dipping sauce for cold soba noodles, or indeed for any kind of noodle – cold, warm or hot. **Serves 4**

2–3 tablespoons lime juice (about 2 limes)
2 teaspoons brown sugar
½ teaspoon sea salt
2–4 bird's-eye chillies, chopped
2 garlic cloves, finely chopped
1 or 2 ripe avocados

❶ Mix all the ingredients except the avocado in a glass bowl.
❷ When you are ready to serve, peel the avocados, dice them and mix them well with the other ingredients.
❸ Divide among 4 bowls and serve.

Rujak sauce

This piquant sauce is very popular in Indonesia and Malaysia. People there use it mainly to dress salads of sour fruit. Recently, however, many Oriental chefs have begun to use it as a sauce for steaks and other grilled meats. Here I recommend it as a spicy dipping sauce for cold soba noodles.
Serves 4 (makes 110 ml / 4 fl oz)

4 tablespoons hot water
60 g / 2 oz grated palm sugar or soft brown sugar
½ teaspoon ready-grilled shrimp paste (page 141)
2 tablespoons lime juice or tamarind water (page 142)
1 teaspoon salt
2–4 bird's-eye chillies, finely chopped
4 spring onions, thinly sliced (optional)

❶ Mix everything except the spring onions in a glass bowl, stirring to dissolve the sugar, shrimp paste and salt.
❷ Divide among 4 small bowls and scatter the sliced spring onion, if using them, over the top.

Soy sauce with chilli

This is widely used in Indonesia and Malaysia – not, in fact, as a dipping sauce for noodles (the way the Japanese prefer), but as a dip for spring rolls and crudités and to add flavour and hotness to noodle and rice dishes. Makes about 6 tablespoons

4 tablespoons light or dark soy sauce
2–6 bird's-eye chillies, finely chopped
1 shallot, finely chopped
1 tablespoon lime or lemon juice
1 teaspoon sugar (if light soy is used)

❶ Mix all the ingredients together in a small bowl.
❷ Use as needed; it will keep in the fridge for up to 7 days.

Nuoc cham (fish sauce with chilli)

Instead of soy sauce, the people of Thailand, Vietnam, Cambodia, Laos – and, to some extent, Burma – prefer fish sauce, called *nam pla* in Thailand and *nuoc mam* in Vietnam. The combination of ingredients for this typical Vietnamese dipping sauce is generally the same as for Soy Sauce with Chilli (above), except for the addition of some grated carrot. Serves 6–8

4 tablespoons fish sauce (*nam pla*, page 140)
2 tablespoons lime or lemon juice
2–6 bird's-eye chillies, chopped
1–2 garlic clove(s), crushed
1 small carrot, grated
1–2 tablespoon(s) chopped coriander leaves

❶ Combine the fish sauce, lime or lemon juice, chillies and garlic in a small bowl. Cover the bowl and refrigerate until needed.
❷ About 1–2 hours before serving, add the grated carrot and chopped coriander leaves and refrigerate again until the moment the sauce goes to the table. (Once the carrots and coriander leaves have been added, the sauce must be consumed on the same day.)

Basic chilli sauce

I include this under the heading of Dipping Sauces because most people in Southeast Asia like to dip almost everything they eat in chilli sauce, from raw vegetables and spring rolls to meat, fish, cooked vegetables, rice and noodles. Because this habit has now spread to the West, we can buy chilli sauces ready-prepared and sold by the jar in Oriental shops and most supermarkets.

The one most widely available is probably *sambal ulek* (which Dutch producers still spell in the old way, '*sambal oelek*'). This is not a brand name, but a description of the sauce, the vital ingredient of which is mashed and pounded chillies. The stuff you buy in shops is good – I often buy it myself – but you can make your own, which is at least as good and costs much less.

Chilli sauce can also be used in cooking. If the recipe requires, say, 2–3 chillies to be blended with other ingredients to make a spice paste, their place can be taken by 1 tablespoonful of this sauce. **Makes 450 ml / ¾ pint**

225–450 g / 8–16 oz large fresh red chillies
1–1½ teaspoon(s) salt
3 tablespoons groundnut oil
1 tablespoon distilled white vinegar or
tamarind water (page 142)

❶ Put the chillies in a large pan of boiling water and cook for 2 minutes. Drain.
❷ Transfer the chillies to a blender, add the other ingredients and blend to the smoothest possible paste.
❸ Transfer this to a saucepan and cook over a low heat for 10–12 minutes, stirring occasionally. Take great care, as the liquid will bubble and spit as it cooks.
❹ Leave the sauce to get cold before storing in an airtight jar. It will keep in the fridge for 3 weeks or longer.

❶ Cook the chillies in boiling water for 2 minutes. ❷ After blending, cook the chilli mixture gently for 10–12 minutes. (Take care, as it will bubble and spit.) ❸ Leave the sauce to get cold before storing in an airtight jar.

dressings

All the dressings in this section are intended to dress cellophane noodles, served with whatever additional ingredients the various recipes describe. Alternatively, the dressings can be used with plain noodles or salads.

Piquant Thai dressing

Thais use more chillies than here; it's a matter of taste. 'Piquant' signifies 'CHILLI HOT'. However, this dressing won't be too hot, even for those unaccustomed to chillies. I use it for all kinds of salad, whenever I want an oil-free dressing. **Serves 4**

2 bird's-eye chillies, finely chopped
2 spring onions, thinly sliced
2 tablespoons chopped coriander leaves
2 tablespoons chopped lemon grass (the inner part only)
1 teaspoon grated palm sugar or soft brown sugar
2–3 tablespoons fish sauce (*nam pla*, page 141)
4 tablespoons lime juice

❶ Mix all the ingredients in a glass bowl.
❷ Refrigerate until needed; it will keep for up to 4 or 5 days.

Piquant dressing with crushed peanuts

Thais love peanuts in salad dressings, not just for their flavour but to add another texture. In fact, they use peanuts in much the same way as Mediterranean cooks use pine nuts. **Serves 4**

2 tablespoons fish sauce (*nam pla*, page 141)
2–4 bird's-eye chillies (red or green), finely chopped
4 tablespoons lime or lemon juice
1–2 garlic clove(s), crushed
1–2 teaspoon(s) finely chopped root ginger
1–2 teaspoon(s) brown sugar or grated palm sugar
60–115 g / 2–4 oz Garlic-flavoured Fried Peanuts (page 45), or any bought roasted peanuts, crushed

❶ Mix all the ingredients except the peanuts in a glass bowl and refrigerate until needed; it will keep for up to a week.
❷ The crushed nuts are sprinkled over the whole salad or noodle dish served with this dressing. Do this just before serving, so they stay crunchy.

Tofu dressing

This dressing also contains sesame seed paste. For best results, make this paste yourself, as below. You can, of course, buy ready-made sesame seed paste from Oriental shops, but be warned, these may contain peanuts. The Middle Eastern paste, tahina (page 142) can also be used for this recipe. **Serves 4–6**

2 tablespoons mirin (page 141)
1 tablespoon soft brown sugar
1 teaspoon salt
3 tablespoons Dashi (page 21) or other stock
1 block Japanese 'cotton' or 'firm silken' tofu (page 142)
2 bird's-eye chillies, finely chopped (optional)
1 tablespoon light soy sauce
2–3 teaspoons lime or lemon juice

for the sesame seed paste:
225–450 g / 8–16 oz sesame seeds

❶ First make the sesame seed paste if making your own: dry-fry the seeds in a frying pan over moderate heat, stirring constantly, for about 3 minutes or until golden brown. Leave to cool.

❷ When cold, pour the seeds into a blender and blend to a smooth paste – just until it becomes a little oily.

❸ Pass this through a sieve if you want your paste to be really smooth. (This is hard work, and you will lose a lot of paste as it sticks to the mesh of the sieve – I prefer my paste slightly coarse anyway.) Keep the paste in an airtight jar in the fridge until needed; it will keep for up to 7 days.

❹ Heat the mirin in a small saucepan for 2 minutes, then add the sugar, salt and stock, stirring to dissolve the sugar and salt. Turn off the heat and leave to cool a little.

❺ When the liquid is cool, pour it into a blender and add the rest of the ingredients, except the lime or lemon juice, with 2 tablespoons of the sesame paste. Blend until smooth.

❻ Transfer the mixture to a glass bowl and refrigerate until needed. Before use, stir the paste with a fork and add 2–3 teaspoonfuls of lime or lemon juice to get the right consistency and to sharpen the flavour.

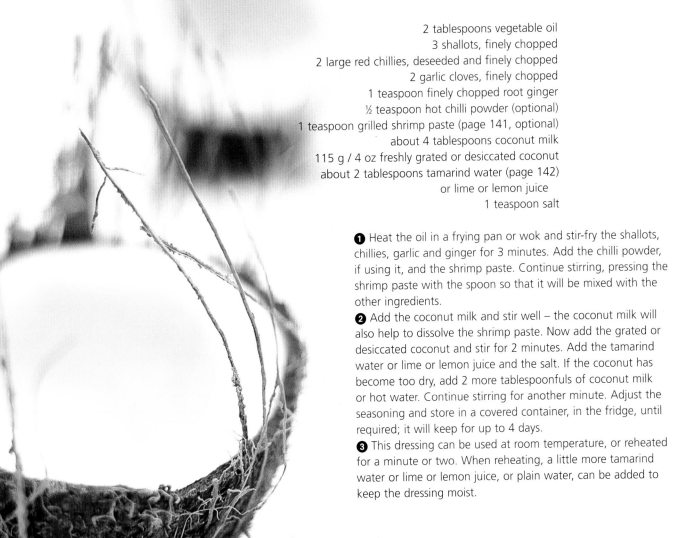

Spicy coconut dressing

Although coconuts are not used for cooking in Japan, Korea or northern China – least of all with noodles – I cannot leave out this dressing. After all, the recipes in this book come from many parts of the globe, and a lot of them use coconut milk, so I recommend that you try coconut as a dressing too. **Serves 4-6**

2 tablespoons vegetable oil
3 shallots, finely chopped
2 large red chillies, deseeded and finely chopped
2 garlic cloves, finely chopped
1 teaspoon finely chopped root ginger
½ teaspoon hot chilli powder (optional)
1 teaspoon grilled shrimp paste (page 141, optional)
about 4 tablespoons coconut milk
115 g / 4 oz freshly grated or desiccated coconut
about 2 tablespoons tamarind water (page 142)
or lime or lemon juice
1 teaspoon salt

❶ Heat the oil in a frying pan or wok and stir-fry the shallots, chillies, garlic and ginger for 3 minutes. Add the chilli powder, if using it, and the shrimp paste. Continue stirring, pressing the shrimp paste with the spoon so that it will be mixed with the other ingredients.
❷ Add the coconut milk and stir well – the coconut milk will also help to dissolve the shrimp paste. Now add the grated or desiccated coconut and stir for 2 minutes. Add the tamarind water or lime or lemon juice and the salt. If the coconut has become too dry, add 2 more tablespoonfuls of coconut milk or hot water. Continue stirring for another minute. Adjust the seasoning and store in a covered container, in the fridge, until required; it will keep for up to 4 days.
❸ This dressing can be used at room temperature, or reheated for a minute or two. When reheating, a little more tamarind water or lime or lemon juice, or plain water, can be added to keep the dressing moist.

pastes

Spicy curry pastes not only form the basis
of many flavourful dishes, they also may
be used as dipping sauces for cold or hot
noodles, or even to flavour a stir-fry.

Red curry paste

For the best curry pastes, you need to dry-roast or dry-fry the coriander and cumin seeds before blending them with the other ingredients. Do this in a frying pan or wok, on a medium heat, stirring the seeds constantly, for about 3 minutes. Don't let them get burnt, or they will taste bitter.

The quantities shown here will make about 600 ml / 1 pint of curry paste, a good deal more than you are likely to need at one time. The surplus can be frozen in an ice-cube tray (2 tablespoonfuls to each cube) and stored in the freezer for up to 3 months; the cubes are ready for use any time as instant curry paste. Alternatively, the paste will keep fresh in the fridge for 7–10 days, if stored in an airtight jar.

Makes about 600 ml / 1 pint

5–10 large red chillies, deseeded and chopped
1 red sweet pepper, deseeded and chopped (optional)
8 shallots, chopped
8 garlic cloves, chopped
1 lemon grass stalk (inner part only), chopped
1-cm / ½-inch piece of galangal (page 140), peeled and chopped
3 kaffir lime leaves, shredded (optional)

3 tablespoons roasted coriander seeds, crushed
3 teaspoons roasted cumin seeds, crushed
3 tablespoons tamarind water (page 142), or lime or lemon juice
3 tablespoons vegetable oil
1 teaspoon salt
1 teaspoon brown sugar

1 Put all the ingredients in a blender with 115 ml / 4 fl oz cold water and blend until smooth.

2 Transfer the mixture to a saucepan. Bring to the boil, lower the heat and simmer gently for 40 minutes.

3 Leave the paste to get cold, then store it in a covered jar in the fridge for up to 10 days until required. Alternatively, you can freeze the paste in ice-cube trays as described above. Transfer the frozen cubes to a plastic bag and keep in the freezer until needed.

Green curry paste

This classic Thai green curry paste is a very versatile mixture which is particularly useful if you keep a supply of it frozen in ice-cube trays, as described for Red Curry Paste on the previous page. You can use it as a dipping sauce for cold or hot noodles, to flavour stir-fried vegetables (see the recipe on page 54) or simply to make a traditional Thai green curry with chicken, or with prawns or lobster, to be eaten accompanied by plain rice noodles. **Makes about 600 ml / 1 pint**

6 tablespoons coriander seeds
2 tablespoons cumin seeds
10 garlic cloves, chopped
2-cm / 1-inch piece of peeled galangal (page 140), finely chopped
2 tablespoons groundnut or vegetable oil
4–6 green chillies, chopped
2 green sweet peppers, deseeded and chopped
225 g / 8 oz shallots, chopped
2 teaspoons shrimp paste (page 141)
115 g / 4 oz bunch of coriander (including leaves, roots and stems), trimmed and chopped
2 lemon grass stalks (inner parts only), chopped
juice of 2 limes (about 3 or 4 tablespoons)
2 teaspoons sea salt

❶ Roast the coriander and cumin seeds in a dry frying pan over a moderate heat, stirring constantly, until they are just becoming brown and fragrant.

❷ Put the roasted seeds into a food processor together with the garlic cloves, chopped galangal and the oil and process for 1 minute. Add the remaining ingredients together with 4 tablespoons of water and process for 3 minutes to get a smooth, free-flowing paste.

❸ Transfer the paste to a saucepan. Heat to just below the boil and simmer gently for 5–8 minutes, stirring often. Add 300 ml / ½ pint hot water and bring to the boil. Cover the pan and simmer gently for 40 minutes, until the paste is quite thick but still flows freely.

❹ The paste is now ready to use, or to be stored in the fridge or freezer as described for the Red Curry Paste on the previous page.

Stages in making and storing curry pastes:
❶ Process all the ingredients together for a minute, then add a little water and process for 2 or 3 minutes more until you have a smooth, free-flowing paste. **❷** Transfer to a saucepan and cook at a very gentle simmer for about 40 minutes. **❸** Leave the paste to get cold in the pan and then store in the fridge or pour it into ice-cube trays for freezing in convenient 2-tablespoon blocks.

Paste for laksa

The name 'laksa' is understood everywhere now to mean a spicy noodle soup made with coconut milk. The original dish, from Malaysia, is called *laksa lemak*, meaning 'delicious laksa' or 'rich-tasting laksa' (see the recipe on page 72). The word 'laksa' itself means rice vermicelli, fine rice noodles. However, I know many chefs in Australia, London and elsewhere, who are familiar with this noodle soup but make it with egg noodles, udon or even soba noodles. Maybe they think their Western customers prefer these to vermicelli; maybe the customers themselves think this. Well, all these kinds of noodle are suitable for laksa, though my preference is for the finer types. What matters most is to recognize and be able to make coconut milk of the right consistency. I shall say more about this in the introductions to some of my laksa recipes.

Laksa paste, like curry paste, can be made well in advance and stored in the fridge for up to 7 days. It can be frozen in an ice-cube tray or small self-sealing plastic freezer bags. It's a good idea to label these clearly and indelibly, and to write the date on them – especially if you are storing a collection of pastes in your freezer. **Makes about 300 ml / ½ pint**

4–6 large red chillies, deseeded and chopped
6 shallots, chopped
3 garlic cloves, chopped
6 candlenuts (page 140), or 10 blanched almonds, chopped
2 teaspoons chopped root ginger
2 teaspoons chopped galangal (page 140)
2 tablespoons coriander seeds, coarsely crushed
½ teaspoon shrimp paste (page 141, optional)
1 teaspoon salt
3 tablespoons tamarind water (page 142)
2 tablespoons groundnut or vegetable oil

❶ Put all the ingredients in a blender or food processor and process for 1 minute, then add 175 ml / 6 fl oz cold water and continue processing for 2 more minutes.
❷ Transfer the smooth paste to a saucepan and cook at just above simmering point for 40 minutes.
❸ Leave the paste to get cold and store as described above. Use as required, and in the quantities given in the recipes.

relishes and dry condiments

All of the condiments in this section have good strong
flavours of their own, but their real point is that they
provide the crisp, crunchy texture that delights all
Asians – as it does anyone who enjoys good food.

Crisp-fried green cabbage leaves

This 'seaweed' appears only twice in this book – as a garnish for Fried Noodles on Portobello Mushrooms (page 53) and in the Braised Duck on Seaweed and Rice Noodles (page 96). It can, however, be used with many recipes and, indeed, with a multitude of dishes that are beyond the scope of a book about noodles. Make just as much as you need, as it won't keep – the shreds don't stay crisp for more than about 30 minutes. The same treatment can also be given to shredded celeriac.

vegetable oil, for deep-frying
2–3 cabbage leaves (the green outer leaves are best), finely shredded and patted dry

❶ Heat the oil in a wok or deep-fryer to 180°C/350°F and put in the shredded cabbage. Stir-fry for 2 minutes, then scoop out with a slotted spoon and put to drain on absorbent paper. This first frying can be done well in advance. A second frying is needed to make the cabbage really crisp.

❷ When you are ready to serve, heat the oil again and fry the cabbage for 1 minute. Drain, and use immediately as a garnish. It will become crisp as it cools.

Crisp-fried dried anchovies

These are another very popular Southeast Asian snack also used as a garnish. Many Western cooks are unfamiliar with them, however, and don't know how to cook them. They must be fried very crisp, and served and eaten before they have time to become the least bit soft or stale. In an airtight container, they should stay in peak condition for 4 days or more. Do not refrigerate them! When buying the anchovies, look for the ones without heads which are sold in many Oriental food stores labelled *ikan teri* (Indonesian) or *ikan bilis* (Malaysian). If you can buy them only with heads still on, cut off and discard these before frying. Makes about 350 g / 12 oz

450 g / 1 lb dried anchovies
225 ml / 8 fl oz or more groundnut oil or corn oil

❶ Heat the oil in a wok to 180°C/350°F and deep-fry the anchovies in two batches for 3 minutes each batch, stirring often. Using a slotted spoon, transfer them to a tray lined with kitchen paper.

❷ For real crispness, you need to fry them a second time for 1–2 minutes. Make sure they do not start to burn.

❸ Leave them to get cold, then store in airtight containers.

Crisp-fried shallots or onions

These are a very popular garnish all over Southeast Asia. They are also widely available ready to use from supermarkets and some delicatessens, usually packed in plastic tubs. For once, I can recommend the commercial product – they are as good as home-made and will save you time and trouble. **Makes about 115 g / 4 oz**

225 ml / 8 fl oz vegetable or groundnut oil
450 g / 1 lb shallots or onions, thinly sliced

1 Heat the oil in a wok and deep-fry the shallots or onions in two batches, stirring often, for 6–8 minutes each, or until golden in colour. Lift them out with a slotted spoon, drain on absorbent paper and leave them to get cold.
2 Store in an airtight jar (not in the fridge) for up to 24 hours until needed.

Crisp-fried noodles

The best noodles for crisp-fried garnish are rice vermicelli, fine egg noodles or somen. They'll all, however, stay crisp only for 30 minutes at most after frying.
Makes about 30 g / 1 oz

60 g / 2 oz rice vermicelli, fine egg noodles or somen
vegetable oil, for deep-frying

1 Soak the noodles in warm water for 3–5 minutes. Drain well and spread them on a tray. Pat dry with kitchen paper.
2 Heat the oil in a wok or a deep-fryer and fry the noodles, a little at a time, for 2–3 minutes, stirring them constantly. Scoop them out and drain on kitchen paper.
3 Crumble them and use as garnish immediately, before the food goes to table.

Garlic-flavoured fried peanuts

Several recipes in this book require crushed peanuts as a garnish. The following method of frying peanuts is by far the best – not just for garnishes, but to eat as a snack with drinks and to make peanut sauce. You can now buy large peanuts with the reddish outer skins already removed. Use these, and fry a good big batch of them – they will keep fresh in an airtight jar for up to a month, if you can keep people from eating them for that long. **Makes about 450–900 g / 1–2 lb**

450–900 g / 1–2 lb peanuts
1.75 litres / 3 pints boiling water
4 garlic cloves, crushed
2 tablespoons sea salt
vegetable oil, for deep-frying

❶ Put the peanuts in a bowl, pour enough boiling water into the bowl to cover the nuts and stir in the crushed garlic and salt. Cover and leave the nuts to soak for 45–60 minutes.
❷ Strain the nuts and discard the soaking water. Spread the nuts on a tray and pat them dry with kitchen paper.
❸ Heat about 600 ml / 1 pint of oil in a wok or deep-fryer. When hot (about 180°C/350°F), fry the nuts in several batches for 4–5 minutes each, stirring them frequently. With a slotted spoon or perforated scoop, transfer the cooked peanuts to a tray lined with kitchen paper.
❹ Leave the peanuts to get cold, then put them in airtight containers for storage. If you store them in glass, keep them in a dark place. Use as described above.

Blushed tomatoes

This is the fancy name given by delicatessens to tomatoes that have been cooked in the oven. The price of them can also be quite fancy, so it is worth making your own if you can spare the time. If you are using tomatoes with thick, tough skins, then skin them first; otherwise, leave the skins on. **Makes about 1 kg / 2 lb**

4 tablespoons chopped flat-leafed parsley
1 tablespoon chopped dill (optional)
1 tablespoon chopped oregano
2–4 garlic cloves, crushed
1–2 teaspoon(s) sugar
1–2 teaspoon(s) sea salt
½ teaspoon cayenne pepper or freshly-ground black pepper
3–4 tablespoons olive oil
about 1 kg / 2 lb tomatoes, peeled (optional, see above) and cut into halves (or quarters if large)

❶ Preheat the oven to 120°C/250°F/gas ½.
❷ In a bowl, mix together all the ingredients except the tomatoes. Taste and adjust the seasoning.
❸ Place the tomato halves or quarters in a single layer in a large ovenproof dish or dishes. Spoon the oil and herb mixture over them, cover loosely with foil and bake in the oven for 1½–2 hours until softened and lightly charred.
❹ Let them get cold and then store in airtight jars. Use as needed; the tomatoes will keep, in their jars in the fridge, for up to a week.

Cucumber relish

This relish is very popular all over Southeast Asia, and each country has its own version. This is the basic relish, but you can make it into Thai cucumber relish by adding 1 tablespoon of fish sauce (*nam pla*, page 140) and some chopped coriander leaves. **Serves 6–8**

1 medium cucumber, peeled and cut in half lengthwise
2–6 bird's-eye chillies, finely chopped
2 tablespoons white distilled vinegar
1 tablespoon sugar
1 tablespoon chopped spring onions or chives

❶ Remove the seeds from the cucumber halves with a teaspoon, then slice the cucumber thinly into half-moon shapes.
❷ Mix these and all the other ingredients together in a bowl, and keep in a cool place for at least 10 minutes before use. The relish can be refrigerated for up to 48 hours before it becomes stale.

VEGETARIAN NOODLES

Noodles with roasted aubergines and tomatoes

Narrow ribbon or round rice sticks (page 10) are my first choices for this dish. The preliminary slow roasting of the aubergines and tomatoes is well worth the extra time in the oven – during which they need no attention whatsoever – as it makes them taste wonderful. The rest of the preparation and cooking take almost no time at all. The result is a vegetable dish that is full of flavour and character, and is good at lunch, dinner or even on a picnic, accompanied by a green salad.
Serves 4 as a light meal

1 aubergine, cut in half lengthwise and then cut into slices about 5 mm / ¼ in thick
8 red or plum tomatoes, skinned, quartered and deseeded
115 ml / 4 fl oz olive oil
2 garlic cloves, crushed
3 tablespoons chopped chives or spring onions
1 tablespoon chopped oregano or basil
1 teaspoon sugar
1 teaspoon fine salt
225 g / 8 oz narrow ribbon or round rice sticks, precooked as described on page 14
6–8 anchovies in oil, chopped
3 tablespoons chopped parsley
½ teaspoon freshly ground black pepper

① Preheat the oven to 120°C/250°F/gas ½. Arrange the sliced aubergines and quartered tomatoes in a large ovenproof dish. Mix the oil, garlic, chopped chives or spring onions, oregano or basil, sugar and salt thoroughly in a bowl, then pour this over the aubergines and tomatoes. Cover the dish with foil and put in the oven. Leave it, undisturbed, for 1½–2 hours. This roasting can be done at any time; if you let the tomatoes and aubergines cool and store them in an airtight jar in the fridge, they will stay fresh for up to a week.

② Reheat the noodles as described on page 16. Put them into a large bowl and, while they are still hot, add the chopped anchovies and parsley. Season with pepper and mix well.

③ If necessary, reheat the roasted aubergines and tomatoes in a frying pan. Taste and add more salt if necessary.

④ To serve: divide the noodles between 4 warmed dinner plates. Top with the aubergines and tomatoes – with, of course, the oil they were cooked in. This dish can be eaten hot, warm or cold.

Fine egg noodles with scrambled tofu

As I write, Chinese fine egg noodles are still not readily obtainable in most supermarkets, but you can use angel-hair pasta instead if you wish. Somen noodles would be equally suitable.

Serves 4 as a light lunch

1 block of fresh Chinese tofu or
2 blocks of firm Japanese tofu
4 tablespoons melted clarified butter or sunflower oil
4 spring onions, sliced thinly into rounds
2 teaspoons finely chopped root ginger
¼ teaspoon chilli powder
2–3 large eggs, lightly beaten

1 tablespoon light soy sauce
salt and freshly ground black pepper
450 g / 1 lb young spinach leaves
¼ teaspoon freshly grated nutmeg
225–340 g / 8–12 oz fine egg noodles,
 precooked as described on page 14
plenty of coriander leaves, to garnish

❶ If using fresh Chinese tofu, rinse it well, then drain it and cut it into small dice; the firm Japanese tofu simply needs to be diced.

❷ Heat 3 tablespoons of the clarified butter or oil in a wok and stir-fry the spring onions, ginger and chilli powder for 2 minutes. Add the diced tofu and continue stir-frying for 2 minutes more.

❸ Add the beaten egg and soy sauce. Stir and scramble the tofu with the eggs. Season with salt and pepper. Turn off the heat and cover the wok.

❹ Heat the remaining clarified butter or oil in a saucepan, then put in the spinach leaves, with some salt and the nutmeg. Stir, cover the pan and let the spinach cook for 2 minutes.

❺ Reheat the noodles as described on page 16 and divide them equally between 4 warmed plates or bowls. Mix the spinach in with the scrambled tofu and arrange on top of the noodles.

❻ Serve immediately, garnished with coriander leaves and with some soy sauce or Basic Chilli Sauce (page 33) in small bowls by each plate so that people can add them as they wish.

Basic fried noodles

The possible accompaniments to fried noodles are endless – practically any grilled meat or fish, for a start. Char-siu pork (page 140), Peking duck (page 139) or any combination of stir-fried vegetables, would be among my first choices. You could also try them with curry.

You can freeze basic fried noodles for up to 2 months. Defrost them completely before you heat them, well covered with foil, in a conventional oven preheated to 180°C/350°F/gas 4 for 5–8 minutes. With a microwave oven, cover them with paper instead of foil and heat on full power for 3 minutes.

Serves 4 as part of a main course

2–3 tablespoons groundnut or sunflower oil	1 tablespoon tomato purée
4 shallots or 1 medium-sized onion, thinly sliced	salt
4 carrots, diced	¾ teaspoon ground white pepper
225 g / 8 oz button mushrooms, quartered	4 tablespoons hot water or chicken stock
2 garlic cloves, thinly sliced	225–350g / 8–12 oz fresh or dried egg
1 teaspoon thinly sliced root ginger	noodles, precooked as described
2 tablespoons light soy sauce	on page 14
1 teaspoon ground coriander seeds	3 spring onions, sliced thinly into rounds

1 Heat the oil in a wok or a large non-stick saucepan and stir-fry the shallots or onion in it for 1 minute. Add the carrots and mushrooms and continue stir-frying for another 2 minutes.

2 Add all the other ingredients except the noodles, hot water or stock and spring onions. Continue to stir-fry for 2–3 minutes more to give the carrots time to cook.

3 Add the hot water or stock, turn up the heat and add the noodles. Stir and toss these on the high heat until the noodles are hot. Add the spring onions and stir again. Taste and adjust the seasoning.

4 Transfer everything to a warmed bowl or serving platter and serve immediately.

Fried noodles on Portobello mushrooms

There are so many different ways of presenting fried noodles, even if you do not use meat. This simple vegetarian dish uses the big Portobello mushrooms as if they were edible plates, with the noodles piled high on top of them. The result is delicious, but you should eat this as soon as it's cooked. Try to time the operation so that the noodles, mushrooms and vegetables all finish cooking at the same moment.

Serves 4 as a first course

4 large Portobello mushrooms, stalks removed
2 teaspoons olive oil
salt and freshly ground black pepper
2 tablespoons groundnut oil
3 shallots, thinly sliced
1 garlic clove, crushed
1 large red chilli, deseeded and sliced thinly at an angle
1 teaspoon chopped root ginger
3 cabbage leaves, coarsely shredded
1 teaspoon ground paprika
1 tablespoon tomato purée

2 tablespoons light soy sauce
3 tablespoons hot water
2 carrots, cut into ribbon slices
   with a potato peeler
110–175 g / 4–6 oz dried egg noodles,
   precooked as described on page 14
handful of Crisp-fried Green Cabbage
   Leaves (page 43)
handful of flat-leafed parsley or
   coriander leaves, to garnish

❶ Preheat the oven to 180°C/350°F/gas 4. Brush the mushrooms with olive oil and sprinkle the open caps with salt and pepper. Arrange the mushrooms on the rack of a baking tin, and bake them in the preheated oven for 20–25 minutes. Time this so that the mushrooms are ready at about the same time as the noodles and the vegetable mixture.

❷ Heat the groundnut oil in a wok or a large saucepan, add the shallots, garlic, chilli and ginger, and stir-fry for 2 minutes. Add the cabbage, paprika and tomato purée, and continue stir-frying for 2 minutes more.

❸ Add the soy sauce and water. Stir once, cover the wok or pan, lower the heat and leave to simmer for 2 or 3 minutes.

❹ Uncover the wok or pan and add the carrots and noodles. Stir the whole mixture around, increasing the heat as you stir, and scooping and stirring the noodles, for about 2 minutes so that the noodles heat through. Taste and adjust the seasoning.

❺ To serve: put each mushroom on a warmed dinner plate, gills upward. Spoon the noodles and the vegetable mixture into the mushrooms, piling them high. Garnish with the crisp-fried cabbage and parsley or coriander leaves. Serve at once.

Timbale of fried noodles and spinach with green curry sauce

This simple but very tasty first course gives a new look to Oriental fried noodles. The only special equipment you need is four ring moulds. Serves 4 as a first course

6–8 tablespoons (or 3–4 frozen cubes) Green Curry Paste (page 40)
450–675 g / 1–1½ lb young spinach leaves
salt and freshly ground black pepper
2 tablespoons Greek-style yoghurt
1 teaspoon cornflour, dissolved in 2 tablespoons cold water
225 g / 8 oz dried egg noodles, precooked as described on page 14
2 tablespoons corn or vegetable oil

2 shallots, chopped
1 garlic clove, chopped
2 teaspoons finely chopped root ginger
large pinch of cayenne pepper
1 tablespoon light soy sauce
1 tablespoon tomato purée
2 tablespoons Crisp-fried Shallots (page 44), to garnish
handful of coriander leaves or flat-leafed parsley, to garnish

❶ Heat half the curry paste in a pan. When hot, stir it with a wooden spoon and add the spinach. Cover for 1 minute. Add a little salt and, with a slotted spoon, transfer the spinach to a sieve. Put over a bowl and press the spinach down with the back of the spoon so that the liquid which is forced out is caught in the bowl.

❷ Pour the liquid from the bowl back into the pan and add the remaining curry paste. In a bowl, whisk the yoghurt with the cornflour paste until smooth. Add this to the pan, stir the mixture and turn off the heat. Adjust the seasoning with salt and pepper if necessary. Set aside until ready to serve.

❸ Prepare to fry the noodles: heat the oil in a wok, add the shallots and garlic, and stir-fry for 2 minutes. Add the remaining ingredients except noodles and garnishes, and stir-fry for another minute, then turn off the heat.

❹ Reheat the noodles (see page 16) and drain them well. Heat the shallot mixture in the wok for 1–2 minutes. Add the reheated noodles and stir and turn them until the noodles and other ingredients are all well mixed. Taste and adjust the seasoning again if necessary.

❺ Just before serving, heat the curry sauce on a low heat, stirring frequently, for 1–2 minutes.

❻ To serve, place a ring mould on the centre of each of 4 plates. Divide the noodles into 4 portions and put half a portion in each mould. Press them down a little with the back of a spoon. Then put equal portions of spinach on top of the noodles, followed by the remaining noodles on top of the spinach, once more pressing them down gently with a spoon. Lift off the moulds and pour the curry sauce around the moulded noodles and spinach. Garnish with Crisp-fried Shallots and coriander leaves or flat-leafed parsley. Serve immediately.

Root vegetables with egg noodles

Not long ago, I ate fresh pasta with baby vegetables in a restaurant that claimed to serve 'modern British food'. The basic ingredients were all right, but the sauce was too buttery and too creamy. My sauce for this recipe is, therefore, based on yoghurt.
Serves 4 as a main course

2 tablespoons extra-virgin olive oil
225 g / 8 oz red onions, thinly sliced
115 g / 4 oz carrots, cut into julienne strips
2 large red chillies, deseeded and thinly sliced
115 g / 4 oz parsnips, cut into julienne strips
115 g / 4 oz celeriac, cut into julienne strips
4 tablespoons chopped flat-leafed parsley
115 g / 4 oz cooked beetroot, cut into julienne strips
½ teaspoon salt
350–450 g / 12–16 oz dried egg noodles, precooked as described on page 14

for the yoghurt sauce:
8 tablespoons Greek-style yoghurt
1 teaspoon cornflour, dissolved in
   2 tablespoons cold water
1 teaspoon sugar
½ teaspoon cayenne pepper
4 tablespoons hot water
salt and freshly ground black pepper

❶ Heat the oil in a wok or pan, add the onions and stir-fry for 3 minutes, then add the carrots and continue stir-frying for 2 minutes. Add the chilli, parsnip and celeriac, and stir-fry for 2 minutes more. Lastly add the parsley, beetroot and salt. Continue stir-frying for 2 minutes more. Turn off the heat and cover the wok or pan.
❷ Make the sauce: in a bowl, whip the yoghurt and cornflour paste until smooth (to prevent the yoghurt from curdling). Add the sugar, cayenne pepper and hot water. Continue beating the mixture for a minute or two.
❸ Transfer the yoghurt mixture to a saucepan, season with salt and pepper and cook, stirring all the time, over a low heat until the yoghurt is hot.
❹ To serve: reheat the noodles as described on page 16 and divide them between 4 ramekins, pressing them down a little with the back of a spoon. Unmould each batch of moulded noodles in the centre of a plate. Arrange equal amounts of the vegetables around the noodles and spoon the yoghurt sauce over the vegetables. Serve immediately.

Layered rice sticks with tofu, shiitake mushrooms and mange-tout stir-fry with red curry sauce

Noodle bars everywhere are filled with loyal customers who love noodles, want fast food and have been working their way through the menu for years. Those who, like Tampopo, have time and inclination to experiment will often be rewarded. Here is an example of one direction you may find worth exploring – it's a vegetarian dish, but if you eat meat you can substitute slices of meat or fish for the tofu the next time you cook it. Serves 4 as a first course or 2–3 as a light meal

2–3 tablespoons groundnut or sunflower oil
6 shallots, thinly sliced
2 tablespoons Red Curry Paste (or 1 frozen cube, page 39)
225 g / 8 oz fresh shiitake mushrooms, sliced
115–175 g / 4–6 oz fried tofu, cut into 8 pieces
150 g / 5 oz mange-tout peas
3 spring onions, cut at an angle into 4 pieces
225 g / 8 oz rice sticks, precooked as described on page 14

for the red curry sauce:
8 tablespoons Red Curry Paste
   (or 4 frozen cubes, page 39)
4 tablespoons water or stock
½ teaspoon salt
1 teaspoon cornflour, dissolved
   in 2 tablespoons cold water
115 ml / 4 fl oz Greek-style yoghurt
freshly ground black pepper

for the garnish:
Crisp-fried Shallots (page 44, optional)
handful of coriander leaves
   or flat-leafed parsley

❶ First prepare the sauce, as this will keep fresh for hours and can be reheated: put the curry paste in a saucepan, heat and stir for 2–3 minutes. Add the water or stock and the salt. Bring to the boil and cook over moderate heat, stirring often, for 3 minutes. In a bowl, whisk the cornflour paste into the yoghurt (this will prevent the yoghurt from curdling) and add to the pan. Continue to simmer for 5 minutes, stirring often. Adjust the seasoning and turn off the heat.

❷ When you are ready to serve, start the stir-frying: heat the oil in a wok and stir-fry the shallots for 5 minutes, until they are just changing colour. Add the curry paste and stir well to mix. Add the mushrooms and stir again for a minute or two before adding the tofu pieces to the mixture, and keep turning them for 3 minutes. Add the mange-tout, spring onions and more seasoning if necessary. Stir once, cover the wok and continue cooking for 1 minute more. Turn off the heat and leave the wok covered.

❸ Reheat the noodles as described on page 16, then drain them well.

4 To serve: put a small quantity of noodles on the centre of each plate (you can use a ring mould to guide you if you wish). Top this with a spoonful of the tofu mixture, then more noodles, followed by more tofu, then finally more noodles on top. Reheat the sauce and pour it around each pile of layered noodles. Garnish with Crisp-fried Shallots, if you are using them, and coriander leaves or flat-leaved parsley. Serve immediately.

Caramelized shallots and aubergines wrapped in rice paper on spinach with blushed tomatoes

Oven-blushed tomatoes are becoming so popular that you can find them in most delicatessens and good food shops. However, if you make your own – and, better still, if you grow your own – they cost much less and taste better. The recipe is on page 47. Serves 4 as a first course

2 tablespoons extra-virgin olive oil
2 teaspoons caster sugar
12 shallots, halved
salt
3 tablespoons olive oil
1 onion, thinly sliced
2 aubergines, cut in half lengthwise, each half sliced into 8–10 pieces
½ teaspoon chilli powder
2 tablespoons chopped parsley

115 ml / 4 fl oz chicken or vegetable stock or hot water
1 tablespoon clarified butter
675–900 g / 1½–2 lb young spinach
freshly ground black pepper
large pinch of freshly grated nutmeg
8 rice paper discs (page 13)
115–175 g / 4–6 oz Blushed Tomatoes (page 47), to garnish

❶ Heat the 2 tablespoonfuls of extra-virgin olive oil in a frying pan, add the caster sugar, and stir until the sugar is melted and lightly coloured. Add the shallots and stir continuously for 4 minutes. Add ½ teaspoon of salt, stir again and turn off the heat.

❷ In another frying pan, heat the 3 tablespoonfuls of olive oil and stir-fry the onion for 5 minutes. Then add the aubergines and continue stir-frying for a minute or two. Add 1 level teaspoon of salt, the chilli powder, parsley and stock. Stir well, cover the pan and simmer for 20 minutes. Check after about 10 minutes and add more stock or water if necessary.

❸ While the aubergines are cooking, heat the clarified butter in a saucepan and cook the spinach, stirring it in the butter and adding salt, pepper and nutmeg to taste. Cover the pan for 2 minutes. Then turn off the heat.

❹ When you are ready to serve, put some hot water into a large bowl. One at a time, dip the rice paper discs into the water for 20–25 seconds each. Put each wet, and now pliable, rice paper on a tray and pat it dry with a kitchen towel. Spread half a portion of aubergine on the rice paper, followed by some caramelized shallots. Roll up the rice paper, leaving both ends of the roll open. Repeat with the remaining rice paper discs.

❺ Divide the spinach between 4 plates. Lay 2 rice-paper rolls on each portion of spinach, garnish with blushed tomatoes and serve at once.

Vegetarian udon casserole

Choose five different vegetables from among those you like best. Prepare them, as described here, well in advance. The actual cooking time will be very short. If you are not vegetarian, use good chicken stock instead of water and serve this casserole as a vegetable side dish, to be eaten with a main course of meat, poultry or fish. **Serves 3–4 as a one-bowl vegetarian meal, or 4–6 as a vegetable side dish**

450 g / 1 lb carrots, peeled and cut into sticks
350 g / 12 oz broccoli, separated into florets
350 g / 12 oz pak choy, cut in half lengthwise
2 tablespoons groundnut oil
1 teaspoon sesame oil
3 shallots, finely chopped
115 g / 4 oz fresh shiitake mushrooms, stalks removed and thinly sliced
225 g / 8 oz chestnut mushrooms, stalks removed and thinly sliced
freshly ground sea salt and black pepper
350 g / 12 oz Chinese cabbage, coarsely shredded
350 g / 12 oz udon noodles, precooked as described on page 14

for the spiced broth:
2 tablespoons light soy sauce
2 teaspoons sugar
2 garlic cloves, crushed
½ teaspoon chilli powder
2 tablespoons finely chopped spring onions
225 ml / 8 fl oz hot water
1 tablespoon sesame paste or tahina (page 142)

① In separate pans of boiling salted water, blanch the carrots, broccoli and pak choy briefly, drain and then refresh in cold water.

② Make the spiced broth: mix all the ingredients in a saucepan and bring to a simmer, stirring constantly until the sesame paste has dissolved. Taste and adjust the seasoning with more soy sauce if necessary.

③ Heat the oils in a heatproof casserole and stir-fry the shallots for 3 minutes. Add the mushrooms and continue stir-frying for 2 more minutes. Season with salt and pepper, then turn off the heat.

④ Now arrange the cooked vegetables in the casserole. Imagine that the space in the casserole is a cake, cut into five equal slices, but with a hole in the middle for the udon noodles. Push all the mushrooms towards one side of the casserole, so they become the first 'slice', and away from the centre. Arrange the carrots next to them, then the Chinese cabbage, then the broccoli. The pak choy goes on the other side of the mushrooms, so that your 'cake' is complete. Pile the udon in the central area.

⑤ Slowly pour the broth all over the vegetables and the noodles, disturbing them as little as possible. Cover the casserole and put it to cook over a moderate heat for 4–5 minutes.

⑥ Serve immediately, as hot as possible, and let everyone help themselves from the casserole.

Soba noodle soup with shiitake mushrooms and tofu

This is an excellent soup to start a vegetarian meal or to come before a main course of fish or meat. Guests who think they don't like tofu will love it when it is cooked this way; the sophisticated manner of its preparation and presentation will win them over before they even taste it. **Serves 4**

30 g / 1 oz white miso (see page 141)
2 teaspoons mirin (see page 141)
115 g / 4 oz firm tofu, cut into 4 slices
salt
1 small aubergine, sliced lengthwise into 4 thin slices
1 tablespoon flour, for dusting
groundnut oil, for deep-frying
115 g / 4 oz fresh shiitake mushrooms, sliced

freshly ground black pepper
600 ml / 1 pint Vegetable Stock (page 23)
1 tablespoon shoyu (see page 142)
1 teaspoon ginger juice (see page 140)
225 g / 8 oz soba noodles, precooked as described on page 14 and drained
2 tablespoons thinly sliced spring onions

1 On a small plate and using a small spoon, mix the miso with 1 teaspoonful of the mirin. Coat the slices of tofu with the softened miso and set aside.

2 In a bowl, dissolve 1 teaspoon of salt in 600 ml / 1 pint of cold water and soak the slices of aubergine in this for 5 minutes to soften them. Then dry them well with kitchen paper.

3 Wrap each miso-coated slice of tofu in a slice of aubergine. Secure each roll with a wooden cocktail stick. Sprinkle the rolls with flour and deep-fry them in hot oil for 3 minutes. Drain them on kitchen paper.

4 Sauté the shiitake mushrooms in a little of the groundnut oil, stirring constantly, for 2 minutes. Season them with a little salt and pepper and drain on kitchen paper.

5 Heat the stock until it is almost boiling. Add the shoyu, the ginger juice and the remaining teaspoonful of mirin. Taste and adjust the seasoning.

6 Reheat the soba noodles as shown on page 16. Divide the noodles between 4 soup bowls, gathering and folding each portion in the bottom of the bowl so that the noodles look neat and tidy.

7 Divide the shiitake mushrooms equally between the 4 bowls. Pour the broth into the bowls. Discarding the wooden cocktail sticks, place a tofu and aubergine roll in the centre of each bowl and top them off with sliced spring onions. Serve at once, piping hot.

Avocado and tofu tempura in miso soup with soba

My younger son, who loves avocado and tempura, commented that if I want this to be considered healthy food I should leave both of them out. Tofu and miso, he said, are good for you, of course, but not everyone likes them. I admit they may be acquired tastes, but most people who try them acquire the taste remarkably quickly. Tofu is rich in proteins, and miso is said to bring down high blood pressure. So while you learn to love miso soup, its benefits will justify your enjoyment of tempura-fried tofu and avocado. Serves 4–6

1–2 ripe avocado(s)
vegetable oil, for deep-frying
1 block of fresh Chinese-style tofu, quartered,
and each quarter quartered again
(16 pieces in all)
225–350 g / 8–12 oz soba noodles, precooked
as described on page 14
6 spring onions, cut into very thin rounds,
to garnish

for the tempura batter:
2 egg yolks
450 ml / 16 fl oz ice-cold water
450 g / 1 lb plain flour
¼ teaspoon salt

for the miso soup:
750 ml–1.1 litres / 1¼–2 pints
   Basic Miso Stock (page 23)
1 tablespoon sake (see page 141)
2 teaspoons mirin (see page 141)
1 teaspoon light soy sauce
¼ teaspoon freshly ground black pepper

❶ First make the tempura batter in two bowls: put an egg in each bowl. Whisk the egg yolk in each bowl, adding half the ice-cold water to each bowl as you do so. Sift half the flour and salt into each bowl and stir gently, with a fork or a pair of chopsticks. Don't beat the batter; it is supposed to be a bit lumpy.

❷ Peel the avocado(s), cut them in half and remove the stone. Cut each half across into 6–8 slices and put them at once into the batter in the first bowl. Do not put the tofu into the batter at this stage.

❸ Heat the oil in a wok or deep-fryer and fry the batter-coated avocado slices, 4–6 slices at a time, for about 2 minutes, turning them over once. Take them out and drain them on kitchen paper. When you are finished with the avocado, start frying the tofu pieces, dipping them one by one into the batter in the second bowl and frying them as you did the avocado slices.

❹ When you are ready to serve, reheat the noodles as described on page 16. Divide them between 4–6 bowls.

❺ Make the soup: heat the miso stock in a saucepan and add all the remaining ingredients. When hot, pour the soup over the noodles in the bowls, and top with the avocado slices, then the tofu pieces. Garnish with spring onions and serve at once.

Coconut, tofu and pumpkin noodles

This is a vegetarian version of a recipe given to me by my Canadian food-writer friend Nathan Fong of Vancouver. His original recipe is for a noodle soup with coconut, pumpkin and prawns, and he uses a chicken stock. You may prefer to follow him rather than me, but being fond of vegetarian dishes myself I have chosen vegetable stock and tofu. Ribbon rice sticks are a good choice to go with this soup. Serves 6–8 as a one-bowl meal

3–5 tablespoons groundnut oil
350–450 g / 12–16 oz Chinese-style fresh tofu, cut into 16 cubes
2 tablespoons Red Curry Paste (page 39)
850 ml / 1½ pints Vegetable Stock (page 23)
1 can (about 280 ml / ½ pint) thick coconut milk
400 g / 14 oz pumpkin (peeled weight), cut into cubes
2 teaspoons chopped lemon grass, the soft inner part only
2 kaffir lime leaves

4 spring onions, cut into thin rounds
2 young celery stalks and leaves, roughly chopped
1 tablespoon Thai fish sauce (*nam pla*, page 140)
225 g / 8 oz rice sticks, precooked as described on page 14

for the garnish:
2 tablespoons Crisp-fried Shallots (page 44)
½–1 teaspoon chilli flakes (optional)
handful of coriander leaves

❶ Heat the oil in a non-stick frying pan and fry the tofu cubes in two batches, turning them over after 2 minutes, then frying them for 2 more minutes on the other side. Drain on kitchen paper and set aside.

❷ Heat the curry paste in a large saucepan, stirring continuously, for 3 minutes. Add the stock and coconut milk. Bring the mixture to the boil and add the pumpkin cubes. Continue cooking over a moderate heat for 10 minutes, or until the pumpkin is cooked.

❸ Add the tofu and the remaining ingredients except the rice sticks and garnishes, and continue to simmer for a further 5 minutes. Taste and adjust the seasoning if necessary by adding more fish sauce or salt.

❹ Reheat the rice sticks as described on page 16. Drain, and divide them between 6–8 warmed bowls. Pour equal amounts of soup, with tofu and pumpkin pieces, over the rice sticks in each bowl. Top with the garnishes and serve very hot.

Spring rolls

Spring rolls, in many different shapes and fillings, have been popular snacks throughout Asia for years, if not centuries. They originated in China, some time before the 6th century AD, when they consisted of pancakes rolled up and filled with the new season's spring vegetables, a welcome change from long winter months of preserved foods. Today's spring roll wrappers are thin sheets of pastry, not pancakes, and the range of fillings is enormous. This recipe is for cooked vegetables, but by all means add minced pork, chicken or prawns if you wish. **Makes 20 rolls**

20 frozen spring roll wrappers, 20–25 cm / 8–10 inches square, defrosted
white of 1 egg, lightly beaten
vegetable oil, for deep-frying

for the filling:
3 tablespoons groundnut or sunflower oil
450 g / 1 lb carrots, cut into matchstick strips
115 g / 4 oz white cabbage, shredded
200 g / 7 oz (drained weight) canned bamboo shoots, rinsed and cut into thin sticks

150 g / 5 oz fresh shiitake mushrooms, stalks removed and thinly sliced
225 g / 8 oz button mushrooms, thinly sliced
2 teaspoons finely chopped root ginger
3 tablespoons light soy sauce
85 g / 3 oz cellophane vermicelli, soaked in hot water for 5 minutes, drained, and cut into approximately 5-cm / 2-inch lengths with scissors
6 spring onions, cut into thin rounds
pinch (or more) of chilli powder

❶ Make the filling: heat the oil in a wok or frying pan, then stir-fry the carrots, cabbage and bamboo shoots in it for 2 minutes. Add both kinds of mushroom, the ginger and soy sauce, and stir-fry for a further 3 minutes. Add the noodles and spring onions and stir-fry on a high heat for 2 minutes, so that the liquid evaporates but the vegetables are still moist. Season to taste with chilli powder. Remove the mixture from the pan and leave it to cool.

❷ Place a spring roll wrapper on a flat surface, so that one corner is pointing at you. Put 2 tablespoons of the filling on this corner. Press the filling down a little, and roll the corner of the wrapper over it, away from you and towards the centre. Fold in the two corners that lie to your left and right. Brush the far corner of the wrapper with a little egg white and roll it up to make a neat cylindrical, well-sealed parcel. Repeat with the rest of the filling and the wrappers, making your spring rolls as nearly even in weight and shape as possible.

❸ Heat the oil in a deep-fryer, wok or pan to 180°C / 350°F. Put 4 spring rolls at a time into the oil, turn down the heat a little and deep-fry for 6–8 minutes, turning them several times, until they are golden brown. Remove them with a slotted spoon and drain on absorbent paper.

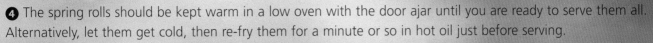

4 The spring rolls should be kept warm in a low oven with the door ajar until you are ready to serve them all. Alternatively, let them get cold, then re-fry them for a minute or so in hot oil just before serving.

5 Cooked spring rolls can be frozen for up to 4 weeks and reheated straight from the freezer. Heat the oil to 150°C / 300°F and deep-fry the frozen rolls for 6–8 minutes so that the filling is heated right through and the wrapper is crisp. If the oil is too hot, the wrapper will blister before the filling has thawed.

NOODLES WITH SEAFOOD

Chopped prawn and quails' egg wonton soup with cellophane noodles

This is a little fiddly to make, but will whet the appetite for the food to follow. Serves 4 as a first course

8 large uncooked king prawns, shelled and deveined
salt and freshly ground black pepper
2 shallots, finely chopped
1 teaspoon finely chopped root ginger
4 teaspoons light soy sauce
large pinch of chilli powder
12 round or square wonton skins
white of 1 egg, lightly beaten

12 quails' eggs
45–60 g / 1½–2 oz cellophane noodles
about 600 ml / 1 pint beef
  or chicken stock
1 teaspoon mirin (see page 141)
1 tablespoon sake (page 141) or dry sherry
12 mange-tout peas
finely chopped spring onions, to garnish
coriander leaves, to garnish

❶ Toss the prawns with a large pinch of salt, then chop them with a large knife and mix them with the shallots, ginger, half the soy sauce and the chilli powder (or put these ingredients in a blender and blend them together for a few seconds). Transfer to a bowl.

❷ Put one wonton skin on a flat plate or tray and brush round the edges with egg white. Then put a teaspoonful of the minced prawn mixture in the centre of the wonton. Make a depression with your finger in the middle of the minced prawn and break a quail's egg into it. Gather the edges of the wonton skin together to make a bag or purse. The egg white will hold the edges together and seal the bag just above the filling. Repeat this until you have 12 little bags ready to be put into the soup before serving.

❸ Soak the cellophane noodles in hot water for 5 minutes, refresh them under cold running water, then drain them well.

❹ While the noodles are soaking, heat the stock with the mirin, sake or sherry and remaining soy sauce. Bring almost to boiling point. Adjust the seasoning and add the wonton bags. Continue to simmer for 3 minutes, then add the mange-tout peas and cook for 1 more minute.

❺ Divide the drained cellophane noodles between 4 large warmed bowls and put 3 wonton bags and 3 mange-tout peas into each bowl, followed by the broth. Scatter the garnish on top and serve at once, piping hot.

Asparagus tips in clear broth
with crab wonton

The clear broth used here is the asparagus cooking stock, though you can, of course, use chicken or fish stock just as well. The stock needs to be light, however, without too many different concentrated flavours. You want the taste of the crab to predominate in the finished dish. **Serves 4-6 as a first course**

16–20 wonton wrappers
white of 2 eggs, lightly beaten
thinly sliced spring onion and red chilli, to garnish
light soy sauce, to serve

for the broth:
450 g / 1 lb asparagus
2 whole tomatoes
2 celery stalks, each cut into 4 pieces

for the filling:
115 g / 4 oz pork meat with a little fat
225–350 g / 8–12 oz white crab meat
1 teaspoon finely chopped root ginger
1 tablespoon finely chopped spring onion
1 tablespoon finely chopped celery leaf
1 egg
salt and freshly ground black pepper
1 tablespoon light soy sauce

1 To make the broth: trim the asparagus tips off about 6 cm / 2½ inches from the top and set aside. Put the rest of the stalks, the tomatoes and celery into a pan with 1.45 litres / 2½ pints of water. Bring to the boil, cover the pan and simmer for 30 minutes. Then break up the tomatoes and continue to simmer for 5 minutes more. Strain this stock into another pan.

2 Meanwhile, make the filling: chop the pork meat and fat with a cleaver until fine. In a bowl, mix this with the rest of the filling ingredients, except the egg and soy sauce. Knead the mixture for a few minutes, then add the egg, salt and pepper, and soy sauce to taste. Mix all these in thoroughly.

3 Divide the filling into as many portions as you have wonton skins. Put one portion in the centre of a wonton skin. Brush the edges of the skin with lightly beaten egg white, then fold the skin to make a triangle, pressing the edges gently to seal it. Fill the other skins in the same way. (This is not the traditional way to fold wonton, but is the easiest and quickest.) You now have 16–20 filled triangles.

4 Heat 1.4 litres / 2 pints of water in a saucepan, and add 1 teaspoon of salt. Bring this to a rolling boil and drop 8–10 filled wonton into it. Cook for 4–5 minutes and remove with a slotted spoon, putting them in a colander to drain. Cook the remaining wonton in the same way.

❺ Just before serving, bring the broth to the boil. Taste, and adjust the seasoning. Add the asparagus tips and simmer for 4–5 minutes until they are just tender.

❻ Meanwhile, divide the wonton between 4 soup bowls and garnish with spring onion and chilli slices. Pour the broth into the bowls, with the asparagus tips divided equally. Serve piping hot. Instead of salt and pepper, let people help themselves to some light soy sauce from a small jug or pourer.

Laksa lemak

This is the original laksa recipe, used to make the spicy noodle soup with coconut milk that was my own family favourite when I was a child in Java. We usually made it with rice vermicelli, slices of chicken breast, prawns and fried tofu.

Serves 8 as a first course or 4 as a one-bowl meal

1.1 litres / 2 pints Basic Chicken Stock (page 24)
8 tablespoons (4 frozen cubes) Paste for Laksa (page 41)
16 uncooked king prawns, heads removed and deveined
1 can (280 ml / 10 fl oz) coconut milk
2 chicken breasts (from making chicken stock above), thinly sliced
salt and freshly ground black pepper

225–350 g / 8–12 oz rice vermicelli, rice sticks or egg noodles, precooked as described on page 14
115–175 g / 4–6 oz fried tofu (page 142), sliced thinly
115 g / 4 oz beansprouts
4 tablespoons thinly sliced spring onion
handful of flat-leafed parsley
2 tablespoons Crisp-fried Shallots (page 44)

❶ Heat the chicken stock in a large saucepan. Add the laksa paste, bring to the boil and simmer for 5 minutes. Add the prawns and cook for 2 minutes. With a slotted spoon, take out the prawns and set them aside in a bowl.

❷ Add the coconut milk and bring the soup almost back to boiling point. Lower the heat a little and let it simmer for 15 minutes, stirring often. Add the chicken slices. Taste and adjust the seasoning with salt and pepper if necessary. Let the soup simmer while you arrange the other ingredients in the serving bowls.

❸ Reheat the noodles as directed on page 16. Drain them and divide them between 4–8 bowls. Put the prawns and fried tofu slices on top of the noodles, followed by the beansprouts and spring onion. Pour the hot soup into the bowls, making sure that the slices of chicken breast are evenly distributed.

❹ Garnish with parsley and Crisp-fried Shallots and serve immediately.

Laksa with udon, scallops and quails' eggs

Good fish stock, with beautifully cut carrots and a coconut milk soup of just the right consistency, make this laksa irresistible. In the introduction to Paste for Laksa on page 41, I stressed the importance of getting your coconut milk just right. I have often been served laksa where the stock was delicious but when I got to the bottom of the bowl I found the coconut milk cooling rapidly and almost solid. This shows that the coconut milk has not been cooked at all. It is fine to use coconut milk from a can, but it must be heated so that it is cooked further before it is eaten. This is how to make coconut milk soup as it should be.

Serves 4 as a first-course soup or 2 as a one-bowl meal

8 quails' eggs
600 ml / 1 pint Basic Fish Stock (page 21)
6 tablespoons (or 3 frozen cubes)
Paste for Laksa (page 41)
350 ml / 12 fl oz coconut milk
2 medium carrots, peeled and cut into thin flower petals

8 scallops, with their corals
salt and freshly ground black pepper
225 g / 8 oz udon noodles, precooked as described on page 14
handful of coriander leaves, to garnish

1 Put the quails' eggs into a small pan of cold water, bring to the boil and boil for 4 minutes, then cool in cold water. Peel and cut in half.

2 Heat the fish stock in a large saucepan. When it starts to boil, stir in the laksa paste and simmer for about 5 minutes. Add the coconut milk and simmer for 10 minutes more, stirring often. Add the carrots and cook for 4 minutes. Add the scallops and continue to simmer for not more than 3 minutes. Adjust the seasoning.

3 Reheat the udon noodles as described on page 16. Divide the noodles between 2–4 warmed bowls. Put the quails' egg halves on top, and pour the laksa soup over the noodles, making sure that each bowl gets an equal share of the scallops and carrots.

4 Garnish with coriander leaves and serve immediately.

Laksa with hot seafood pot

I recommend this particular laksa to anyone who lives where seafood is abundant and can be bought really fresh. The best noodles to go with it are rice vermicelli, which should be served and eaten in separate bowls, not mixed with the soup. By all means use chopsticks to eat the noodles, prawns and fish, but drink the soup from the bowl, Japanese-fashion (though this is not a Japanese dish). For me, this is much more enjoyable than using a spoon; but if you really want to use a spoon, of course, there's no reason at all why you shouldn't. **Serves 4 as a main course**

850 ml / 1½ pints Vegetable Stock (page 23)
6–8 tablespoons Paste for Laksa (page 41)
280 ml / 10 fl oz coconut milk
salt and freshly ground black pepper
175 g / 6 oz monkfish tail fillet
115 g / 4 oz turbot fillet
12 large uncooked king prawns, shelled and deveined
115 g / 4 oz salmon fillet
115 g / 4 oz crab meat (white meat only),
or shelled cooked cockles

juice of 1 lime (about 2 tablespoons)
handful of coriander or basil
    or mint leaves, to garnish
2 red bird's-eye chillies, chopped (optional)
350 g / 12 oz rice vermicelli, precooked
    as described on page 14

❶ Heat the stock in a large saucepan and, when hot, add the laksa paste. Simmer for a few minutes and add the coconut milk. Continue to simmer for 5 minutes, stirring frequently. Taste and adjust the seasoning.

❷ Now add the monkfish fillet and let this simmer for 1 minute before adding (in this order) the turbot, prawns and salmon. The fish can be left whole or broken into portions if you prefer. Continue cooking for 2 more minutes, then add the crab meat or cockles, the lime juice and chillies if using. Bring the soup almost to boiling point, cover the pan and turn the heat off. Serve as soon as you are ready with the noodles.

❸ Reheat the rice vermicelli as described on page 16, drain well and transfer to a large bowl. Moisten the noodles with a little of the soup from the seafood pot.

❹ Give each guest a small bowl and let them help themselves to the noodles. Serve the soup and seafood in somewhat larger soup bowls, garnished with herbs. Eat the laksa and the noodles as described above.

Pan-fried scallops with chicory and apples on parsleyed soba or egg noodles

If you have freshly made soba or egg noodles, they are perfect for this dish, but dried noodles will do very well. Serves 4 as a first course

4 tablespoons clarified butter
about 3 tablespoons extra-virgin olive oil
8–12 scallops, with or without corals
2 apples (preferably Granny Smith or Cox's), peeled, cored and each cut into 8 wedges
16 chicory leaves
large pinch of chilli powder or cayenne pepper

2 tablespoons light soy sauce
1 tablespoon mirin (see page 141)
¼ teaspoon freshly grated nutmeg
salt and freshly ground black pepper
175–225 g / 6–8 oz soba or egg noodles, precooked as described on page 14
115 g / 4 oz flat-leafed parsley, chopped

❶ In a large pan, heat half the clarified butter with the oil. When these are good and hot, fry the scallops, 4 at a time, for 2 minutes, turning them over twice during that time. Transfer them to a warmed plate.

❷ Pan-fry the apple pieces for 2 minutes on each side. Transfer these to a warmed plate.

❸ Add a little more oil if necessary and fry the chicory leaves until wilted. Add the chilli powder, soy sauce, mirin and nutmeg. Put the scallops and apples back into the pan. Season with salt and pepper. Cover the pan, turn off the heat and leave for 1 minute.

❹ Reheat the noodles as described on page 16 and then drain them well.

❺ Heat the remaining clarified butter in a wok, then add the chopped parsley and ¼ teaspoon salt and stir for 1 minute. Add the drained noodles and mix all well together.

❻ Divide the parsleyed noodles between 4 warmed plates and top them with equal portions of scallops, chicory and apples. Serve immediately.

Vietnamese stuffed squid with rice stick noodles

This is a good party dish, hot or cold, with or without noodles; alternatively, you can take it on a picnic. The noodles make a contrast with the bright red beetroot dipping sauce and the flavours go together very well indeed. Soba noodles are also good with this squid.

Serves 8 as a first course or a picnic lunch, or 4 as a main course

8 small prepared squid, about 7 cm / 3 inches long, the tentacles reserved and chopped for the stuffing
vegetable oil, for frying
225–350 g / 8–12 oz rice stick noodles, precooked as described on page 14
4–6 tablespoons Beetroot and Anchovy Dipping Sauce (page 27)

for the stuffing:
60 g / 2 oz cellophane vermicelli, soaked in hot water for 5 minutes, then drained
225 g / 8 oz lean pork, minced
115 g / 4 oz fresh shiitake mushrooms, thinly sliced
4 spring onions, cut into thin rounds
4 garlic cloves, chopped
1 teaspoon finely chopped root ginger
1 large red chilli, deseeded and chopped
2 tablespoons chopped Vietnamese mint or spearmint
1 tablespoon Vietnamese fish sauce (*nuoc mam*, page 141)
large pinch of salt
1 egg, lightly beaten

❶ Prepare the stuffing: using scissors, cut the vermicelli into pieces about 5 cm / 2 inches long. Put these in a large bowl. Add all the remaining ingredients except the egg, including the chopped squid tentacles. Mix well and add the egg, then continue mixing until thoroughly combined.

❷ To fill the squid: spoon some of the stuffing into each one, pressing it down until the squid is about three-quarters full. Close the opening of the squid and secure with a wooden cocktail stick.

❸ Heat about 115 ml / 4 fl oz of oil in a non-stick frying pan and fry the squid, turning them often, for 5 minutes. Using a needle or a fine skewer, pierce them in several places while they are cooking. Then continue frying, turning them often, for a further 5–6 minutes or until they are golden brown.

❹ Remove the squid from the pan and lay on a tray lined with kitchen paper to drain. Remove the cocktail sticks. Leave the squid to cool a little then, with a sharp knife, slice each one diagonally into 3 or 4 pieces.

❺ Reheat the noodles as described on page 16 and serve immediately, with the Beetroot Dipping Sauce and the sliced squid.

Sichuan prawn chow mein

I have been asked many times why I have never put a chow mein recipe in any of my books. Chow mein simply means 'fried noodles', so evidently the time has come to produce this recipe, which otherwise I would simply have called 'Sichuan prawn fried noodles'. **Serves 4 as a one-bowl meal**

24 large uncooked king prawns, shelled, cut in half lengthwise and deveined
salt
125 ml / 4 fl oz groundnut oil, for frying
4 shallots, finely chopped
2 teaspoons finely chopped root ginger
1 teaspoon sugar
2 garlic cloves, very thinly sliced
4 spring onions, cut into thin rounds
1 teaspoon Sichuan pepper (see page 142), crushed in a mortar with a pestle until fine, or 1 teaspoon chilli powder

1 tablespoon Chinese rice wine or dry sherry
1 tablespoon soy sauce
3 red tomatoes, skinned and chopped
½ teaspoon freshly ground black pepper
225–350 g / 8–12 oz egg noodles, precooked as described on page 14
2 tablespoons chopped coriander leaves

1 Rub the halved prawns with ½ teaspoon of salt and keep them in the fridge while you prepare the spice mixture.

2 Heat 2 tablespoonfuls of groundnut oil in a wok. Fry the shallots and ginger for 2 minutes. Add the sugar and garlic, and stir-fry for 1 minute more. Then add the remaining ingredients, except the oil, noodles and prawns, together with more salt to taste. Continue stir-frying for 2 more minutes.

3 Heat the rest of the oil in a frying pan and, when hot, fry the prawns, stirring them all the time, for about 2 minutes. Remove them with a wire scoop and transfer to a tray lined with kitchen paper.

4 Reheat the noodles as described on page 16. Stir them into the contents of the wok and mix well. Add the fried prawns and coriander leaves, and go on stir-frying for 1 minute longer. Serve immediately.

Singapore fried noodles

There are endless versions of this dish, which is also widely known in the West by its Chinese name, *char kwee teow*. As a rule, the noodles are rice noodles – narrow or wide ribbons, rice sticks or rice vermicelli. Whichever type you choose, I recommend that you toss the noodles with the meat and prawn mixture just before serving. **Serves 4 as a one-bowl meal**

2 tablespoons groundnut oil
3 shallots, chopped
2 garlic cloves, chopped
2 teaspoons finely chopped root ginger
115 g / 4 oz lean pork, cut into julienne strips
1 red chilli, deseeded and chopped
2 tablespoons yellow bean sauce
115–175 g / 4–6 oz brown or shiitake mushrooms, sliced
1 tablespoon light soy sauce

2 teaspoons tomato purée
225 g / 8 oz (about 8–12) uncooked prawns, shelled, cut in half lengthwise and deveined
225–350 g / 8–12 oz rice sticks, precooked as described on page 14
115 g / 4 oz crab meat
4–6 spring onions, sliced at an angle
salt and freshly ground black pepper
handful of flat-leafed parsley

❶ Heat the oil in a wok or a wide saucepan, then stir-fry the shallots, garlic and ginger for a minute or two. Add the pork and continue stir-frying for 3 minutes. Now add the chopped chilli and yellow bean sauce, and stir well to mix everything. Add the mushrooms, soy sauce and tomato purée. Continue cooking, stirring constantly, for 1 minute. Add the prawns and go on stir-frying for 2 minutes more.
❷ After adding the prawns, reheat the noodles. Drain them well and transfer them to a large bowl.
❸ Continue stir-frying the meat and prawn mixture for 1 minute (3 minutes in total), and add the crab meat and spring onions. Stir once, taste and adjust the seasoning.
❹ Transfer the meat and prawn mixture to the bowl containing the noodles. Toss to combine everything well together and garnish with the parsley. Serve immediately.

Burmese fish soup with rice stick noodles

This is a good party dish which can quite easily be cooked in double quantities and put on the buffet for guests to help themselves from a big steaming bowl. The accompaniments can be arranged on an adjacent large plate. For a one-bowl meal to serve, say, 4 people, you can give each person a bowl of soup and a plate of bits and pieces alongside.

The accompaniments can be prepared a little while in advance – they do not have to be hot when they come to table, but the soup must be. Banana flowers may sound exotic, but they can be bought in many Asian shops; if you can't find one, use canned palm hearts, which are easy to find.

Serves 4 as a one-bowl meal

1 tablespoon groundnut oil
2 shallots, thinly sliced
2 garlic cloves, thinly sliced
1 red chilli, deseeded and thinly sliced
½ teaspoon finely chopped root ginger
5-cm / 2-inch stem of lemon grass, outer leaves discarded and the soft inner part finely chopped
450 ml / ¾ pint coconut milk
225 g / 8 oz monkfish tail, filleted and cut into 4 pieces
225 g / 8 oz salmon fillet, cut into 4 pieces
600 ml / 1 pint Basic Fish Stock (page 21)
salt and freshly ground black pepper

for the accompaniments:
1 banana flower, the 2 outer layers discarded, or 225 g / 8 oz canned palm hearts
225 g / 8 oz rice stick noodles
2 hard-boiled ducks' or hens' eggs, peeled and quartered, or 6–8 quails' eggs, peeled and halved
1–1½ tablespoons chopped flat-leafed parsley
Crisp-fried Onions (page 44)
Basic Chilli Sauce (page 33)

1 Prepare the accompaniments: if using banana flower, boil it whole in lightly salted water for 6–8 minutes. Drain it, cut it into four quarters, then slice these across fairly thickly. If using palm hearts, drain off the liquid, rinse and drain again, then slice them quite thickly. Put the banana flower or palm hearts on one side of the serving dish or plate. The rice noodles are simply heated as described on page 16 and put in the centre of the dish. The eggs, parsley and onions also go on the dish, and the chilli sauce is served in its own bowl or bowls.

2 To make the soup, heat the oil in a good-sized saucepan. Stir-fry all the solid ingredients except the fish for 2 minutes. Add the coconut milk, bring to the boil and add the monkfish and salmon. Simmer for 2 minutes. Add the fish stock. Continue heating through for about 1 or 2 more minutes. Adjust the seasoning and serve immediately.

Caramelized cod fillet on rice vermicelli with yard-long beans in spicy coconut dressing

This caramelized fish is Thai in origin, but the yard-long beans in their coconut dressing take me back to my childhood – even at six years old I liked hot chillies. Thailand and Indonesia share a fondness for rice noodles. Of course, if there were no noodles in the kitchen cupboard, we were perfectly happy to eat our fish and beans with plain boiled rice. **Serves 4 as a one-bowl meal**

4 cod fillets, each weighing about 150–175 g / 5–6 oz
1 tablespoon lime juice
½ teaspoon salt
450 g / 1 lb yard-long beans, cut into 5-cm / 2-inch lengths
¼ measure of Spicy Coconut Dressing (page 37)
3–4 tablespoons demerara sugar

225 g / 8 oz rice vermicelli, soaked in hot water as described on page 14 and well drained
60 g / 2 oz Crisp-fried Dried Anchovies (page 43, optional), to garnish

1 Rub the cod fillets all over with lime juice and salt. Leave in a cool place while you do the rest of the preparation.

2 Boil the beans in slightly salted water for 4 minutes, then drain and refresh in cold water. Drain again.

3 In the rinsed-out saucepan, mix the beans with the coconut dressing. Heat gently, stirring them around with a wooden spoon for a minute or two until they are just warm.

4 Spread the demerara sugar on a plate and coat the cod fillets all over with it.

5 Preheat the grill while you reheat the noodles as described on page 16. Drain them well.

6 Grill the fish for 2–3 minutes on one side, turn them over and grill the other sides for a further 3 minutes.

7 Divide the noodles between 4 plates. Put a piece of fish on top of each helping and spread a portion of beans and coconut around it. If you are using them, sprinkle the anchovies over all. Serve warm.

Tea-smoked monkfish with rice sticks and rujak sauce

I find this dish really great fun to make and I am always very pleased with the result. However, it does take a little time. The way to tackle it is to do most of the preparation well in advance, a day ahead if you can; then, on the day itself, you can bring this noodle dish to table in less than 10 minutes. Serves 4 as a main course

575 g / 1¼ lb monkfish tail fillet, in 2 pieces
1 tablespoon fine sea salt
115 g / 4 oz plain flour
115 g / 4 oz soft brown sugar
3 tablespoons black tea-leaves
(Assam, Darjeeling or Oolong)
350–450 g / 12–16 oz rice sticks (the
narrow-ribbon kind), precooked
as described on page 14

2 measures of Rujak Sauce (see page 30)
1 green apple, peeled, cored and diced
1 small, not-quite-ripe mango,
peeled and diced
115 g / 4 oz watercress, trimmed

❶ Well ahead, ideally the day before, prepare the monkfish for smoking: rub the fish fillet all over with the salt and leave in the fridge for at least 2 hours, or overnight. Rinse off the salt under cold running water and dry well by patting with kitchen paper.

❷ Use a thick-bottomed saucepan with a tight-fitting lid or a wok with a domed lid, lined with a double thickness of aluminium foil. On the foil, spread the flour, sugar and tea. Place a wire rack over these and lay the fish on the rack. Cover the pan or wok tightly and put it over a moderate heat for 6 minutes. Then turn the fish over and continue smoking for another 6 minutes. Transfer the fish to a plate and set aside.

❸ When you are ready to serve, reheat the noodles, drain them well and put them in a warmed bowl. Cover the bowl to keep the noodles warm.

4 Pour a measure of the Rujak Sauce into a frying pan and heat gently. Cut each piece of fish in half (making 4 portions altogether) and place these side by side in the warm sauce. Leave them there for 1 minute, then turn them over and continue cooking for another minute. Turn off the heat and cover the pan.

5 Put a slice of fish in the centre of each of 4 warmed plates. Arrange the apple, mango and watercress on top of the fish, letting some pieces fall to the side. Toss the noodles with the sauce from the pan and arrange them around the fish. Serve warm.

6 Serve the remaining Rujak sauce in 4 small bowls as an extra dipping sauce.

NOODLES WITH POULTRY

Indonesian chicken soup with rice noodles

Chicken soup is as highly regarded in Indonesia as it is everywhere else. You can, of course, serve it with rice instead of noodles. Serves 6–8 as a first course or 4 as a one-bowl meal

1 small chicken, cut into 4
1 teaspoon salt

for the garnish:
225 g / 8 oz rice noodles, precooked
as described on page 14
115 g / 4 oz beansprouts
1 tablespoon chopped flat-leafed parsley
1 tablespoon chopped spring onion
4 or 8 lemon slices
2 tablespoons Crisp-fried Shallots (page 44)

for the paste:
6 shallots or 1 large onion, chopped
3 garlic cloves, chopped
2.5-cm / 1-inch piece of root ginger,
peeled and chopped
3 candlenuts (page 140) or 5 blanched
almonds, chopped
¼ teaspoon ground turmeric
½ teaspoon chilli powder
2 tablespoons groundnut or olive oil
2 tablespoons hot water

❶ Bring 1.4 litres / 2½ pints water to the boil in a large pan. Add the chicken pieces and the salt, and simmer for 50 minutes, skimming as necessary.

❷ Put all the ingredients for the paste in a blender and blend for a few seconds only. Transfer this rough paste to a bowl and set aside.

❸ When the chicken is cooked, strain off the stock and reserve. When the meat is cool enough to handle, shred it into small pieces, discarding the fat but keeping the bones.

❹ Put the paste from the bowl into a clean saucepan and heat it, stirring all the time, for 3 minutes. Add the chicken bones and half the stock, cover the pan and simmer for 15 minutes.

❺ Strain the stock into another saucepan and add the rest of the stock. Return to the boil and simmer for 15 minutes, skimming if necessary. Add the chicken meat and simmer for another 5 minutes.

❻ To serve as a one-bowl meal: reheat the cooked rice noodles as described on page 16 and divide between 4 warmed bowls. Divide the rest of the garnish (except the fried shallots) between the bowls and ladle the hot soup and chicken pieces over them. Sprinkle the fried shallots over all and serve at once.

Chicken dumpling soup with butternut squash and udon

The main ingredients of this dish are enhanced by a hot-and-sour broth, for which I find Paste for Laksa (page 41) particularly suitable. The thick coconut milk is optional; the soup is still very good without it. You can use any type of squash in season, preferably one with a good yellow colour for contrast to the pale soup. To add colour and extra flavour to my chicken dumplings, I put pistachio nuts in the mixture. **Serves 6–8 as a first course or 4 as a one-bowl meal**

2 tablespoons lemon juice
salt and freshly ground black pepper
1.1 litres / 2 pints chicken stock
4 tablespoons Paste for Laksa (page 41)
175–225 g / 6–8 oz peeled butternut, Thai or
other yellow squash, cut into small cubes
4–8 tablespoons very thick coconut milk (optional)
1–2 tablespoon(s) lime juice (or more lemon juice)
115–225 g / 4–8 oz udon noodles, precooked
as described on page 14
handful of coriander leaves, to garnish

for the dumplings:
60 g / 2 oz shelled pistachio nuts
2 skinless chicken breast fillets, diced
¼ teaspoon salt
¼ teaspoon chilli oil (page 140)
1 teaspoon ginger juice (page 140)
1 teaspoon light soy sauce
white of 1 egg, lightly beaten

❶ Prepare the dumplings: in a small pan of water, boil the pistachio nuts for 2 minutes, drain and, when cool enough to handle, peel off the skins. Put the nuts and all the other dumpling ingredients except the egg white in a blender and blend for a few seconds. Transfer to a bowl, add the egg white and stir with a fork or wooden spoon in one direction only for 2 minutes. Chill for 20–30 minutes.

❷ I like my dumplings small (so that they can be easily picked up with chopsticks or in a soup spoon), so divide the chicken paste into 3 portions, roll each portion on a sheet of foil to make a sausage shape about 1 cm / ½ inch in diameter, or a little thicker, and cut each sausage at an angle into dumplings about 2 cm / ¾ inch long.

❸ Bring about half a panful of water to the boil and add the lemon juice and some salt. Plunge a few dumplings into the boiling water and leave them for 6–8 minutes, then scoop them out with a slotted spoon and set aside in a bowl. Repeat until all your dumplings are boiled.

❹ Heat the stock in a saucepan with the laksa paste and simmer for 3 minutes. Add the coconut milk, if using it. Bring almost to the boil again, then add the squash and cook for 5 minutes until this is tender. Add the lime or lemon juice, taste and adjust the seasoning. Add the dumplings and continue cooking for 2 more minutes.

❺ When ready to serve, reheat the noodles as described on page 16. Arrange the noodles in the bowls and ladle the soup, squash and dumplings over the noodles. Serve piping hot, garnished with the coriander leaves.

Egg noodles with chicken and shiitake mushrooms

Fine egg noodles or angel-hair pasta are suitable for this recipe. It's a very practical dish, as everything can be prepared well in advance. You could quite easily use the cooked chicken left over from making the chicken stock on page 24.

Serves 4 as a first course or 2 as a one-bowl meal

4 skinless chicken breast fillets, sliced very thinly across the grain
2 tablespoons groundnut or vegetable oil
115 g / 4 oz fresh shiitake mushrooms, sliced
1 teaspoon finely chopped root ginger
4 spring onions, sliced thinly at an angle
225 g / 8 oz fine egg noodles or angel-hair pasta, precooked (page 14) and drained
2 tablespoons light soy sauce
2 teaspoons sesame oil
1 teaspoon chopped garlic
salt and freshly ground black pepper
handful of coriander leaves, to garnish

for the marinade:
1 tablespoon sake (see page 141) or dry sherry
1 teaspoon light soy sauce
1 teaspoon mirin (see page 141) or honey
¼ teaspoon cayenne pepper
2 teaspoons lemon juice

1 Make the marinade by mixing all the ingredients in a glass bowl and add the chicken slices. Mix well and leave the chicken to marinate in the fridge for 30 minutes to 1 hour.

2 At the end of this time, drain the chicken. Heat the oil in a wok or frying pan and stir-fry the chicken for 4 minutes. Add the shiitake mushrooms and ginger, and continue stir-frying for 2–3 minutes more. Mix in the spring onions, stir-fry for 1 minute and remove from the heat.

3 When you are ready to serve, reheat the noodles as described on page 16. Drain them well and transfer to a large warmed serving bowl.

4 Put the soy sauce, sesame oil and chopped garlic into a small saucepan, heat gently for 2 minutes and pour the mixture over the noodles. Toss to mix well, then season with salt and pepper.

5 Reheat the chicken and shiitake briefly, then add these to the noodles and toss again to mix well. Adjust the seasoning and serve, garnished with the coriander leaves.

Chicken wing party noodles

This is a great party dish for older children – say, seven or eight years old and upwards. You can buy chicken wings almost anywhere now, fresh or frozen, in large plastic bags. I recommend buying them fresh, cooking them well in advance and then freezing them. On the day of the party, defrost them, reheat and serve with plain-cooked egg noodles. **Serves 6–8**

1 kg / 2¼ lb chicken wings
3 tablespoons lemon juice
4 garlic cloves, crushed
1 teaspoon salt
3 tablespoons groundnut oil
2 teaspoons chopped root ginger
4 tablespoons chopped spring onions
2 tablespoons dark soy sauce

2 tablespoons light soy sauce
1 teaspoon freshly ground black pepper
2 tablespoons tomato ketchup
1 teaspoon sugar
1.1 litres / 2 pints chicken stock or hot water
450 g / 1 lb dried egg noodles, precooked
  as described on page 14

❶ Put the chicken wings in a large bowl and rub them well with the lemon juice, crushed garlic and salt. Leave them in the fridge for at least 1 hour, or preferably overnight.

❷ When you are ready to cook the wings, heat the oil in a large, heavy-bottomed saucepan. When the oil is hot, put in the chicken wings and stir them around with a wooden spoon for 3–4 minutes. Add the chopped ginger and spring onions, and continue stirring for another 2 minutes.

❸ Add both types of soy sauce, the black pepper, tomato ketchup and sugar. Stir again for a few seconds, then add the chicken stock or hot water. Bring to the boil, lower the heat and cover the pan. Cook for about 30 minutes.

❹ Uncover the pan, adjust the seasoning and continue cooking over a low heat, uncovered, for another 30 minutes, stirring the wings around from time to time. They are now ready, either to be served immediately or to be left to go cold and then frozen.

❺ To serve: reheat the noodles, drain them well and arrange them on a warmed serving platter. Pour the hot chicken wings and their sauce over them. Ask your guests to help themselves. They can eat the wings with their fingers and use forks or chopsticks for the noodles. Remember to put several empty bowls on the table for the bones.

Casserole of noodles with hot-marinated fried chicken

Fried chicken is delicious and all children love it, but I find frying a chicken at the last moment is a hassle. This casserole can be cooked well in advance; it needs only to be reheated over a moderate heat for 7 or 8 minutes. Serves 6–8 as a main course

8 boned chicken thighs, each cut into 4
2 skinless chicken breast fillets, each cut into 4
3 tablespoons plain flour
½ teaspoon salt
¼ teaspoon freshly ground pepper
vegetable oil, for deep-frying
350–450 g / 12–16 oz egg noodles,
or soba or udon
4 spring onions, cut into very
thin rounds, to garnish

for the marinade:
3 tablespoons groundnut or sunflower oil
1 large red onion, finely chopped
1 teaspoon finely chopped root ginger
3–8 small dried or fresh red chillies, left whole
4–6 spring onions, cut into 1-cm / ½-inch lengths
2 tablespoons dark soy sauce
2 tablespoons light soy sauce
115 ml / 4 fl oz brown rice vinegar or red wine vinegar
115 ml / 4 fl oz chicken stock or any other good stock
1 tablespoon sugar (or more, if you like it sweet)
salt and freshly ground black pepper

❶ Several hours ahead, or ideally the day before, prepare the marinade: heat the oil in a pan or wok and fry the onion for 5 minutes over moderate heat, stirring all the time. Add the ginger and chillies, and stir for 1 minute more. Add all the remaining marinade ingredients. Stir for another minute, taste and add a little salt and pepper to taste, if necessary. Transfer to a large bowl and leave to cool.

❷ Coat the chicken pieces with seasoned flour. Heat the oil for deep-frying in a wok or deep-fryer and fry the chicken in 2 or 3 batches, for 6–8 minutes each time, until nicely browned, moving them about in the hot oil from time to time. Scoop out as they are cooked and put straight into the cooled marinade. Turn the chicken over a few times in the marinade, cover and keep in a cool place for at least 4 hours, or overnight in the fridge.

❸ About half an hour before you are ready to serve, if the chicken has been kept in the fridge take it out. While it is coming back to room temperature, cook the noodles as described on page 14.

❹ Put the chicken, with the marinade, in a large casserole and put this over a moderate heat for 5 minutes or until it is just starting to boil. At this point, if you want your casserole to be a little more chilli-hot, take out 2 or 3 whole chillies from the casserole, crush them with the back of a spoon and stir them back in.

❺ Add the precooked noodles, stir well to mix them with the chicken, cover and cook for 2 minutes more.

❻ Serve piping-hot, garnished with the spring onions, letting everybody help themselves from the casserole into large individual bowls.

Chicken wontons with blushed tomatoes

For this recipe I suggest you use round wonton wrappers, not square. The resulting wontons will look very much like ravioli, and if you make fresh pasta you can use your own ravioli pasta instead of wontons. Serves 4 as a first course

1 teaspoon groundnut or olive oil
24 round wonton wrappers
8 pieces of Blushed Tomato (page 46)
Parmesan cheese, extra-virgin olive oil
or soy sauce, to serve

for the filling:
2 tablespoons groundnut oil
1 tablespoon clarified butter
4 tablespoons chopped young leeks
2 garlic cloves, crushed
2 skinless chicken breast fillets, minced
2 teaspoons finely chopped root ginger
4 water chestnuts, finely chopped
large pinch of cayenne pepper
¼ teaspoon finely ground black pepper
½ teaspoon salt
1 teaspoon fish sauce (*nam pla*, page 140)
1 egg

1 First cook the filling: heat the oil and butter in a wok. Stir-fry the leeks and garlic for a minute or two, then add the minced chicken meat. Continue stir-frying for 3 minutes, then add the rest of the ingredients except the egg. Stir-fry for 2 more minutes, then taste and adjust the seasoning. Transfer the filling to a bowl and let it cool. When cold, add the yolk from the egg and mix well. Reserve the egg white for sealing the wontons.

2 To fill the wontons: arrange 6 wonton wrappers in 2 rows of 3 on a flat surface. Brush round the edge of each with the egg white. Put a portion of the filling on each of 3 wrappers, then lay the other wrappers on top to cover the filling. Press the edges well together to seal them. Fill the other wontons in the same way. Lay the stuffed wontons on a tray lined with baking parchment and cover them with a clean damp tea towel.

3 When you are ready to serve, boil about 1.75 litres / 3 pints of water in a large saucepan. Add a pinch of salt and a teaspoonful of groundnut or olive oil. When the water is at a rolling boil, put in 4 stuffed wontons, one by one, and let them cook for 4 minutes. Take them out with a wire scoop and drain them on kitchen paper. Continue cooking the other wontons in the same way.

4 While they cook, heat the blushed tomatoes in a small pan over a low heat. Serve the wontons hot, 3 per person, on warmed plates, with the hot blushed tomatoes. You can, if you wish, grate Parmesan cheese over each serving, as if the wontons were ravioli; alternatively, drizzle them with extra-virgin olive oil or soy sauce.

Braised duck on seaweed and rice noodles

The 'seaweed' used here is the Crisp-fried Green Cabbage Leaves on page 43, but there is no reason why you shouldn't make this dish with real sea-vegetable or sea-spinach, whenever this is readily available. **Serves 4 as a main course**

4 duck breast fillets
2 portions of Crisp-fried Green Cabbage Leaves (page 43) or about 60 g / 2 oz sea-vegetable or sea-spinach
2 tablespoons groundnut oil
850 ml / 1½ pints warmed chicken stock
salt
225 g / 8 oz rice vermicelli, precooked as described on page 14

for the marinade:
2 garlic cloves, crushed
2 teaspoons finely chopped root ginger
1 bird's-eye chilli, finely chopped
1 tablespoon dark soy sauce
1 tablespoon light soy sauce
2 tablespoons lime juice
1 star anise
1 tablespoon groundnut oil

❶ Mix all the ingredients for the marinade in a glass bowl. Slash the skin of each duck breast down to the meat at an angle several times along its length and add them to the marinade. Mix well and leave to marinate in the fridge for several hours or overnight. Take them out of the fridge about 30 minutes before you want to cook.

❷ When ready to serve, prepare the cabbage and keep it warm.

❸ Heat the oil in a deep frying pan and, when it is very hot, sear the duck breasts, skin-side first, turning them over after 2 minutes. Cook the other sides for 2 minutes, then add the marinade and simmer for 5 minutes. Now add the chicken stock, cover the pan and cook for 15 minutes. Turn the duck breasts over once, after 7 or 8 minutes. Uncover the pan and add salt to taste. Continue cooking for 5 more minutes. By this time, the sauce should be quite thick.

❹ Reheat the noodles as described on page 16, then drain and divide between 4 warmed plates. Cut each duck breast at an angle into 4 or 5 slices. Arrange equal portions of cabbage on top of the noodles and the duck slices on top of that. Pour a portion of sauce around (not on) each pile of noodles and serve immediately.

Vietnamese noodle soup with steamed duck

You can make this with duck breast fillets or with the legs from a Peking duck (see page 139) – if using the latter, you do not need to marinate them. Use chicken stock or vegetable stock, not duck stock, as it is too strong in flavour.

Serves 4 as a one-bowl meal

2 whole duck legs or 2 duck breasts (see above)
300 ml / ½ pint groundnut oil or corn oil
1.1 litres / 2 pints chicken or vegetable stock
225 g / 8 oz pak choy or Chinese cabbage, roughly chopped
4 stalks of young celery with the leaves, roughly chopped
2 tablespoons chopped spring onions
225 g / 8 oz rice stick noodles, precooked as described on page 14
salt and freshly ground black pepper
handful of coriander leaves, to garnish

for the marinade (duck breasts only):
2 tablespoons light soy sauce
1 tablespoon honey
½ teaspoon salt
1 tablespoon lemon juice

❶ If using duck breasts: mix all the ingredients for the marinade in a glass bowl and marinate the duck breasts for at least 2 hours or in the fridge overnight. Then drain them and discard the marinade.

❷ Put the duck breasts or legs on a plate and steam them for 20 minutes over boiling water in a large saucepan or steamer set on a high heat. (If you use a saucepan, rest a wire trivet or some other stable heatproof object on the bottom to support the plate. Pour in enough water to provide 20 minutes' steaming, but not so much that it can get on the plate with the duck.) Take out the duck and let it cool.

❸ Fry the duck pieces in oil for 5–6 minutes until nicely browned, drain them and set aside.

❹ Heat the stock in another large saucepan and, when boiling, add all the remaining ingredients except the noodles, seasoning and coriander leaves. Taste and adjust the seasoning. Simmer for 2 minutes.

❺ Meanwhile, slice the duck meat and (if you are using duck legs) discard the bones.

❻ Divide the noodles between 4 bowls and put a portion of the sliced duck meat on top. When you are ready to serve, pour the soup into the bowls, sprinkle with coriander leaves and serve immediately.

Sam Leong's Shanghainese noodles

Sam Leong is the Chinese Chef at the famous Jiang-Nan Chun restaurant in the Four Seasons Hotel, Singapore. This is a new recipe that he has devised, based on a beanstarch sheet. These glassy sheets made from mung bean flour are, he tells me, typical Shanghai products. If you can't get them, use a small amount of cooked glass vermicelli instead. Conpoy are dried scallops, available from specialist Chinese stores. They are expensive, but you need only a small quantity. Crisp-fried, they are used as a garnish. If you can't get them, simply leave them out – there is no satisfactory substitute.

Serves 4 as a first course or 2 as a one-dish light meal

2 skinless duck breast fillets, rubbed with salt and pepper, or 225 g / 8 oz roast duck meat
60 g / 2 oz (or more) conpoy (see opposite, optional), to garnish
125 g / 4 oz green beanstarch sheet (see opposite), soaked in cold water for 1 hour to soften, then drained
12 fresh shiitake mushrooms, stalks removed
1 small celery heart, cut into julienne strips
2 garlic cloves, thinly sliced
3 spring onions, cut at an angle into 2-cm / ¾-inch pieces
60 g / 2 oz beansprouts

for the sauce:
2 tablespoons groundnut oil
2 shallots, finely chopped
2 garlic cloves, finely chopped
1 red chilli, deseeded and finely chopped
1 teaspoon finely chopped root ginger
2 tablespoons chopped celery leaves or flat-leaf parsley
600 ml / 1 pint Basic Chicken Stock (page 24)
2 tablespoons white rice vinegar
2 tablespoons Chinese red vinegar
1 tablespoon Kikkoman soy sauce
1 teaspoon sesame oil
few drops of chilli oil
salt
2 tablespoons chopped spring onions

❶ If you are using uncooked duck breasts, roast them in an oven preheated to 200°C/400°F/gas 6 for 25 minutes, let them rest for 2–3 minutes in a warm place, then slice the meat very thinly. Previously roasted duck (e.g. leftovers of Peking duck) need only be sliced or shredded.

❷ If using conpoy, soak them in warm water for 45–60 minutes, then pat dry, shred and deep-fry until crisp.

❸ Make the sauce: heat the oil in a wok or saucepan and fry the chopped shallots, garlic, chilli and ginger for 2 minutes, stirring continuously. Stir in the celery leaves or parsley, then add the stock. Bring to the boil and simmer for 3–4 minutes. Add the rest of the ingredients for the sauce except the spring onions and simmer for a further 3–4 minutes. Taste and add more soy sauce or salt if necessary. Add the spring onion and set aside.

❹ Cut the softened beanstarch sheet into small rectangular shapes (about half the size of a standard sheet of lasagne). In a small saucepan, heat about 150 ml / ¼ pint of the sauce. When it is almost boiling, heat the beanstarch pieces in the sauce for 1–2 minutes, then take them out, drain and keep warm in a bowl.

❺ Heat 4 tablespoons of the remaining sauce in a wok. When hot, add the shiitake mushrooms, celery heart and sliced garlic. Stir them around for 1–2 minutes. Add the spring onion, beansprouts and the cooked duck meat. Stir-fry for another minute, then add the remaining sauce. Bring to the boil and continue to cook for 2–3 minutes.

❻ To serve: divide the beanstarch pieces between 2–4 bowls and divide the duck meat and sauce equally between them. Garnish with crisp-fried conpoy, if using it, and serve immediately.

Balinese minced duck satays on fried noodles

Fried noodles are a popular alternative to fried rice in Bali and elsewhere in Indonesia. They are usually served with at least one accompanying dish, often a satay such as this one. No sauce is needed here because the spice mixture is already in the minced duck. **Serves 4–6 as a main course**

5–6 skinless duck breasts, minced
Basic Fried Noodles (page 51)

for the spice mixture:
2 shallots, chopped
2 garlic cloves, chopped
½–1 teaspoon chilli powder
1 teaspoon finely chopped fresh
   galangal or root ginger
2 teaspoons coriander seeds
1 teaspoon cumin seeds

2 cloves
½ teaspoon ground cinnamon
½ teaspoon cardamom seeds
½ teaspoon freshly grated nutmeg
½ teaspoon ground turmeric
2 teaspoons chopped lemon grass,
   the inner part of the stalks only
1 teaspoon sea salt
2 tablespoons tamarind water (page 142)
   or lemon juice
2 tablespoons groundnut oil

❶ Put all the ingredients for the spice mixture in a blender and process to a smooth paste. Transfer to a saucepan and simmer, stirring occasionally, for 4–6 minutes. Leave to get cool.

❷ When the paste is cold, mix it well with the minced duck in a glass bowl. Knead the mixture with your hand for a minute or two, then divide into 12–18 portions. Form each portion into a ball, push a skewer through the middle of the ball and mould the meat around the skewer to make a sausage shape. Repeat until you have 12–18 sticks of satay.

❸ Make the fried noodles. At the same time, preheat the oven to 200°C/400°F/gas 6. When it is hot, bake the satays for 15–18 minutes. Alternatively, preheat a hot grill and grill them for 10–12 minutes, turning them several times.

❹ Serve the satays as soon as they are cooked, either on top of or alongside the noodles or with the noodles in separate bowls.

Quail stuffed with noodles and herbs

For this, buy quails that have already been boned or ask your butcher to bone them (try to get them still with the legs). The quails are to be stuffed with herbed noodles then roasted in the oven. The result is deliciously crisp outside, tender and full of flavour within. **Serves 4 as a first course or a light lunch with extra noodles**

4 boned quails
4 tablespoons clarified butter or olive oil
2 tablespoons chopped flat-leaf parsley
2 tablespoons chopped chives or spring onions
2 teaspoons finely chopped garlic
1 tablespoon light soy sauce
115 g / 4 oz fine egg noodles, precooked
as described on page 14

for the marinade:
2 tablespoons clear honey
1 tablespoon lemon juice
1 tablespoon light soy sauce

❶ Mix the marinade ingredients in a glass bowl, add the quails and rub the mixture well into the skin. Leave to marinate for at least 2 hours.

❷ Heat half the clarified butter or oil in a frying pan, add the chopped parsley, chives or spring onions and garlic, and sauté for 2 minutes. Add 1 tablespoonful of soy sauce, then toss the noodles in the herb mixture. Take the pan off the heat and let the noodles get cold.

❸ Preheat the oven to 220°C/425°F/gas 7. While it is heating, stuff the quails with the cold noodles, cramming as much as you can into the body cavity of each. Then make each stuffed quail into a little parcel, held together by string (or sew them up). Don't worry if a few noodles are left hanging out of each parcel; the final cooking will make them nicely crisp.

❹ Sear the quails in the remaining clarified butter or oil in a frying pan, turning them around until they are brown all over. Then place them on a rack and roast them in the oven for 10–12 minutes. Drain them well and leave to rest for 3 or 4 minutes before serving.

❺ To serve: put each stuffed quail on a warmed dinner plate and cut and remove the strings. With a sharp knife, cut each quail in half lengthwise and arrange the two halves to show off the herbed noodles. For a one-dish light lunch, add more cooked noodles.

NOODLES WITH MEAT

Noodle soup with beef and lemon grass

This Vietnamese dish is equally good with or without chillies.

Serves 4 as a one-bowl lunch

2 tablespoons vegetable oil
1 tablespoon tomato paste
1 teaspoon chilli sauce (optional)
1 teaspoon shrimp paste (page 141)
2 shallots, thinly sliced
225 g / 8 oz narrow-ribbon rice sticks,
precooked as described on page 14
1 tablespoon fish sauce (ideally
nuoc mam, page 140)
salt and freshly ground black pepper
1 tablespoon chopped coriander leaves

1 tablespoon thinly sliced spring onions
½ cucumber, peeled, halved lengthwise,
deseeded and sliced
2 Cos lettuce leaves, shredded

for the stock:
2 pork chops, some of the fat trimmed off
225 g / 8 oz chuck steak or brisket, in
2 pieces, some of the fat discarded
1 lemon grass stalk, cut into 3 pieces
½ teaspoon salt

1 Put all the ingredients for the stock in a large saucepan with 1.75 litres / 3 pints cold water, bring to the boil and simmer for an hour or so, skimming off the froth frequently. Take the meat out and leave to get cold. Strain the stock into a large bowl.

2 Slice the pork chops and beef thinly, discarding the bones of the chops. Set the slices of meat aside.

3 In a small bowl, mix the oil, tomato paste, chilli sauce if using it, and the shrimp paste. Transfer the mixture to a large saucepan, put over a moderate heat and sauté for 2 minutes. Add the sliced shallots, stir for a few seconds, then add a ladleful of stock and simmer for 3 minutes. Now add the rest of the stock and continue to simmer for 20 minutes.

4 When you are ready to serve the soup, reheat the noodles as described on page 16 and drain them well. Then heat the stock and add the fish sauce. Taste and adjust the seasoning with salt and pepper if necessary.

5 To serve: divide the noodles between 4 large individual bowls and put equal amounts of the sliced beef and pork on top of them. Sprinkle the coriander leaves and spring onions on top of the meat, then ladle the stock into each bowl. Just before taking the soup to table, float the slices of cucumber and the shredded lettuce on top of each bowl. Serve immediately and eat while hot. Alternatively, put all the soup in a large tureen and let everyone help themselves.

Udon soup with sautéed beef and bamboo shoots

This makes an excellent one-bowl lunch or supper on a cold day. The secret of its fine flavour is to use a really good beef stock. Thinly sliced raw beef is available in Japanese food shops and good supermarkets. **Serves 4 as a one-bowl meal**

2 tablespoons clarified butter
350 g / 12 oz thinly sliced raw beef
60 g / 2 oz dried shiitake mushrooms, soaked in hot water for 10 minutes, then drained and sliced; or 115 g / 4 oz fresh shiitake mushrooms, sliced
115 g / 4 oz canned bamboo shoots, drained and rinsed, then thinly sliced
1 tablespoon light soy sauce
350–450 g / 12–16 oz udon noodles, precooked as described on page 14
4 spring onions, cut into thin rounds

for the broth:
1.1 litres / 2 pints beef stock
1 tablespoon sake (see page 141)
1 tablespoon mirin (see page 141)
1 tablespoon light soy sauce
1 teaspoon ginger juice (page 140)
salt and freshly ground black pepper

❶ Put all the ingredients for the broth except the salt and pepper into a saucepan. Bring to the boil and simmer gently for 10 minutes. Adjust the seasoning with salt and pepper if necessary.

❷ Heat the clarified butter in a non-stick frying pan and sauté the beef for 2 minutes. Add the mushrooms and bamboo shoots and stir them around. Stir in the soy sauce and about 2 tablespoonfuls of the broth. Cover the pan and simmer for 2–3 minutes.

❸ When ready to serve, reheat the udon (see page 16) and the broth, until it is just about to boil.

❹ To serve: divide the udon between 4 large warmed soup bowls. Pour the broth over the udon to cover them and arrange the beef slices, mushrooms and bamboo shoots in equal portions on top of each bowl. Add the spring onion on top or at one side of the bowl and top up the bowls with the remaining stock. Serve piping hot. Use chopsticks to eat the udon and other solids and drink the soup straight from the bowl. (You may, of course, use forks and spoons if you prefer.)

Rack of lamb with asparagus noodles

For this I use the rack of single-rib cutlets from the best end of the neck, which is often sold pre-packed in supermarkets. This is a perfect dish for entertaining as the cutlets and asparagus noodles can be prepared and part-cooked an hour or so in advance; the final cooking, just before serving, is done *en papillote*, with the lamb wrapped in baking parchment or greaseproof paper. Serves 4

12–16 lamb cutlets
½ teaspoon sea salt
1 tablespoon lemon juice
115–175 g / 4–6 oz parsley, finely chopped
16 garlic cloves
350–450 g / 12–16 oz very fine or wild asparagus

4 tablespoons clarified butter (page 140)
   or olive oil
2 teaspoons whole fresh green peppercorns
freshly ground black pepper
225–350 g / 8–12 oz soba noodles, precooked
   as described on page 14

❶ Put the cutlets in a bowl and rub them with the sea salt, lemon juice and chopped parsley. Set aside until you are ready to cook. Peel the garlic cloves and simmer them in a small pan of water for 15 minutes, then drain. At the same time, blanch the asparagus in a pan of lightly salted boiling water for 2 minutes, refresh in cold water and drain well.

❷ When you are ready to cook the lamb, preheat the oven to 200°C/400°F /gas 6 and heat 2 tablespoonfuls of clarified butter or oil in a large frying pan. Fry the cutlets, in two batches, for 2–3 minutes on each side, turning them once. When the second batch have finished frying, take the pan off the heat, put all the cutlets in it together and cover the pan to keep them warm.

❸ Heat the remaining butter or oil in a wok. Add the softened garlic and the asparagus, and stir-fry them for 2 minutes. Then add the green peppercorns and salt and pepper to taste. Finally, put in the precooked soba noodles and stir them for 2 minutes so that everything is well mixed together.

❹ Cut 4 sheets of baking parchment or greaseproof paper to the size and shape of a large dinner plate. Lay the 4 discs of paper on a work surface and divide the cutlets and noodles equally between them, piling them on one half of the disc so you can fold the other half over them to seal the parcel. Make sure that each parcel contains 3 or 4 garlic cloves.

❺ Seal each parcel by folding the paper over the cutlets and noodles and turning the edges as if you were making a Cornish pasty. Put the parcels on a baking tray and cook in the oven for 5–8 minutes. Allow to rest for 2 minutes.

❻ Serve by putting a parcel on each dinner plate and letting people open their own. They should slide the meat and noodles off the paper disc with the aid of a knife and discard the paper.

Black-peppered beef on wok-fried udon

Most supermarket meat counters now sell beef steaks that have been ready-crusted with black pepper, and you can use these if you prefer – but here's how to do it yourself from scratch. **Serves 4**

2 tablespoons whole black peppercorns
1 tablespoon whole white peppercorns
about 1 teaspoon coarse sea salt
1 kg / 2 lb 3 oz rump or sirloin steak, in 4 pieces
1 tablespoon olive oil, if frying

for the noodles:
3 tablespoons groundnut oil
2 shallots, finely chopped
2 garlic cloves, finely chopped
2 tablespoons oyster sauce or dark soy sauce
4 young celery stalks, with leaves, roughly chopped
85–115 g / 3–4 oz beansprouts
1 teaspoon sugar
350–450 g / 12–16 oz udon noodles, precooked
   as described on page 14
4 spring onions, cut into thin rounds, to garnish

❶ Grind the black and white peppercorns and the sea salt together in a mortar, but not too finely. Spread the ground mixture on a flat plate and place the steak on top, then press down hard to encrust the surface of the meat. Turn the steak over and do the same on the other side. Set the steak aside until you are ready to cook it.

❷ Preheat the grill to high and grill the steaks for about 5 minutes on each side, turning them once. Alternatively, heat the olive oil in a heavy-based frying pan, arrange the encrusted steaks side by side and fry over a moderate-to-high heat, for 4–5 minutes on each side, turning them once. You can fry them for up to 2 or 3 minutes longer on each side, if you don't want them pink in the middle.

❸ While the steaks are cooking, prepare the noodles: put the oil in a hot wok and add the shallots and garlic. Stir-fry these for a minute or two, then add the oyster or soy sauce and celery. Continue stir-frying for another 2–3 minutes. Add the beansprouts, sugar and a little salt to taste. Stir for 1 more minute and remove from heat.

❹ Reheat the udon noodles as described on page 16. Put the wok with the stir-fried ingredients over a moderate heat and add the noodles. Stir-fry for 2 minutes so that everything is hot, then arrange on a warmed serving platter.

❺ The steak pieces should now be almost ready to serve. When they are cooked, put them on a wooden chopping board and slice the meat thinly. Arrange the slices on top of the noodles and serve immediately, garnished with spring onion.

Noodles with chilli beef and fried basil

This dish comes from no country in particular, so you can use whatever noodles you choose or happen to have in the cupboard. My own choice would be either soba or fine egg noodles. **Serves 4 as a one-bowl meal**

500–750 g / 1–1½ lb rump steak or sirloin steak, cut into thin strips
18–20 basil leaves
4-5 tablespoons vegetable oil
2 tablespoons mirin (page 141) or dry sherry
350–450 g / 12–16 oz noodles (see above), cooked as described on page14
light soy sauce, to serve

for the marinade:
2–3 large red chillies, deseeded and chopped
4 garlic cloves, chopped
1 teaspoon chopped root ginger
2 tablespoons Thai fish sauce (*nam pla*, page 141)
1 teaspoon sugar
2 tablespoons lime juice or lemon juice
2 tablespoons groundnut oil
salt and freshly ground black pepper
2 tablespoons chopped basil

1 Put all the ingredients for the marinade except the basil into a blender and blend until smooth. Transfer to a glass bowl, mix in the chopped basil and marinate the beef in it for 1–2 hours.

2 Heat the oil in a wok or frying pan and fry the basil leaves for 1–2 minutes, until they become translucent. Leave to cool; when cold, they will be crisp.

3 Discard most of the oil in the wok or pan except for about 2–3 tablespoonfuls. Heat this again and add the beef with the marinade. Stir-fry for 3–4 minutes over a high heat. Splash the mirin over it, then continue stir-frying for 1 minute more only. Adjust the seasoning with salt and pepper if necessary. Turn off the heat and cover the pan.

4 Reheat the noodles as described on page 16. Shake well and divide them between 4 warmed plates or bowls. Top them with equal portions of the beef. Garnish with the fried basil leaves and serve at once. Instead of salt and pepper, put some containers of light soy sauce on the table, so that people can season their noodles for themselves.

Parsleyed egg noodles with lamb kofta in red curry sauce

Kofta **is the Indian name for meatballs. These can be made with any meat you wish, or even with vegetables; my** *kofta* **here are made of lamb and lentils. If you are a vegetarian, try using lentils and butter beans.** **Serves 4 as a main course**

whites of 1–2 eggs, lightly beaten
4 tablespoons plain flour
vegetable oil for frying
350–450 g / 12–16 oz egg noodles, precooked
as described on page 14
2 tablespoons clarified butter
115–175 g / 4–6 oz parsley, chopped
¼ teaspoon salt
Crisp-fried Celeriac (page 43), to garnish (optional)

for the sauce:
6–8 tablespoons Red Curry Paste (page 39)
175–225 ml / 6–8 fl oz coconut milk
salt and freshly ground black pepper

for the kofta:
115 g / 4 oz red lentils
225–350 g / 8–12 oz lean
lamb meat, minced
3 shallots, finely chopped
2 garlic cloves, finely chopped
1 teaspoon chopped root ginger
3 teaspoons ground coriander
½ teaspoon freshly grated nutmeg
2 tablespoons chopped mint, or 1
tablespoon finely chopped fresh rosemary
½ teaspoon cayenne pepper
about 1 teaspoon salt
1 egg, lightly beaten

1 Make the kofta: cook the lentils in boiling water for 5 minutes, then drain. In a bowl, mix them with all the other kofta ingredients and knead the mixture for a minute or two. Mould the mix into meatballs about the size of walnuts. You should end up with 20–30. Chill for 30 minutes to firm them up before frying.

2 When you are ready to fry the kofta (which can be done well ahead of serving), dip each one into egg white and roll in the flour. Heat the oil in a non-stick frying pan or a wok and fry them, 6 or 8 at a time, turning them over several times until they are golden brown. Drain on kitchen paper.

3 Reheat the noodles as described on page 16 and drain them well. In a wok, heat the clarified butter, then add the chopped parsley and salt and stir for 1 minute. Add the drained noodles and mix all well together.

4 Make the sauce: cook the curry paste and coconut milk together in a saucepan for 6–8 minutes, letting this sauce bubble gently over a moderate heat and stirring often. Taste and adjust the seasoning. Just before serving, put the fried meatballs into the sauce for a minute or two to reheat them.

5 To serve, pile equal portions of the parsleyed noodles on 4 plates. Pour the sauce and meatballs over the noodles and scatter the garnish, if using, over all. Alternatively, serve the noodles in one bowl and the meatballs and sauce in another, and let everyone help themselves.

Barbecued pork spare ribs with shiitake noodles

You can eat this as a simple main course or as a one-dish meal. The spare ribs can be prepared well in advance. Serves 6–8 as a one-dish meal or main course

1 teaspoon salt
2 kg / 4½ lb pork spare ribs, cut
into 7–8 cm / 3–3½ in lengths
4 tablespoons oil
8 shallots, finely chopped
2 teaspoons finely chopped root ginger
2 tablespoons dark soy sauce
3 tablespoons light soy sauce
2 tablespoons Hoisin sauce
1 teaspoon sugar
1–2 teaspoon(s) freshly ground black pepper
115 ml / 4 fl oz hot water
3 tablespoons Shaohsing wine
(see page 141) or dry sherry
115 ml / 4 fl oz chicken stock

for the noodles:
350–450 g / 12–16 oz egg noodles,
    precooked as described on page 14
3 tablespoons groundnut oil
1 large red onion, thinly sliced
2 teaspoons finely chopped root ginger
2 garlic cloves, crushed
225–350 g / 8–12 oz fresh shiitake
    mushrooms, stalks removed
    and thinly sliced

1 Preheat the oven to 160°C/325°F/gas 3.

2 Pour 3 litres / 5 pints water into a large saucepan, bring to the boil and add the salt. Stir to dissolve and add all the spare ribs. Simmer for 5 minutes, drain and pat the ribs dry with kitchen paper.

3 Heat the oil in a large casserole. Add the ribs and stir them around for 4 minutes. Then add the shallots and ginger. Continue stirring for another 3 minutes.

4 Add the rest of the ingredients, except the wine or sherry and the chicken stock, increase the heat and cover. Leave over a moderate heat for 3 minutes. Put the casserole in the oven and cook for 1¼–1½ hours.

5 Remove from the oven, turning the oven up to 200°C/400°F/gas 6 if you are going straight on to finish the dish, add the Shaohsing wine or sherry and stir the ribs to coat them with the sauce.

6 Remove the ribs from the sauce and arrange them side by side on a rack in a roasting tin. Transfer the sauce from the casserole to a small saucepan. Up to this point, everything can be done well ahead of serving time – up to 6 hours in advance.

7 Shortly before you are ready to serve, put the ribs in the hotter oven and cook for 10–15 minutes, or until hot. Add the stock to the sauce in the saucepan and heat it gently. Save 4 tablespoonfuls of the sauce for the noodles and use the rest as a dipping sauce to be served with the ribs.

8 To prepare the noodles: reheat as described on page 16 and drain. Heat the oil in a wok and stir-fry the onion, ginger and garlic for 5 minutes. Add the shiitake mushrooms, stir for 2 minutes and add the reserved sauce from the ribs. Continue stir-frying for 2–3 minutes, then add the reheated noodles. Stir-fry for 2 more minutes.

9 Serve the noodles and ribs hot in separate bowls. The noodles and the ribs can be eaten together, or you may prefer to eat the ribs first, with the dipping sauce, and then the noodles as a course by themselves.

Pad Thai

Rice vermicelli, the Thais' favourite noodles, are the best choice for this classic favourite, though I also use very fine egg noodles or angel-hair pasta. Serves 4 as a light lunch, accompanied by a green salad

2 tablespoons groundnut or sunflower oil
4 shallots, thinly sliced
2 garlic cloves, thinly sliced
1 teaspoon finely chopped root ginger
225 g / 8 oz lean pork, sliced thinly across the grain and cut into julienne strips
2 tablespoons Thai fish sauce (*nam pla*, page 141) or light soy sauce
300 ml / ½ pint hot water
salt and freshly ground black pepper
225–350 g / 8–12 oz fine egg noodles, precooked as described on page 14

175–225 g / 6–8 oz watercress leaves
handful of coriander leaves

for the garnish:
115 g / 4 oz Garlic-flavoured Fried Peanuts (page 45)
60 g / 2 oz dried shrimps (see page 141), soaked in hot water for 10 minutes, then drained
1 teaspoon crushed chillies
pinch of salt

❶ First prepare the garnish: put the fried peanuts in a food processor and switch it on for 2 seconds only. The nuts should be only very roughly chopped. Remove and set aside. Repeat this two-second processing with the shrimps and chillies together. Put the processed shrimps and chillies into a non-stick frying pan and dry-fry for 1–2 minutes, stirring all the time. Leave to cool, then put them in a jar and add the chopped peanuts with a little salt. Mix together with a spoon and put the lid on; this mix will keep fresh for a few days if the jar is kept airtight.

❷ When you are ready to serve, cook the pork mixture: heat the oil in a wok or a large shallow saucepan. Add the shallots, garlic and ginger, and stir continuously with a wok scoop or spoon for 2 minutes. Add the pork and continue to stir-fry for 2 more minutes. Add the fish sauce or soy sauce and hot water, stir once, cover the pan and simmer for 4–5 minutes.

❸ Uncover the pan, increase the heat and let the mix bubble for 2–3 minutes, stirring occasionally. Taste, and add some salt if necessary, and pepper. Stir again, until all the cooking juices are absorbed by the meat, but taking care that the mixture remains quite moist.

❹ While the pork is cooking, reheat the noodles as described on page 16. Loosen the noodles by hand and add them to the mix. Stir them around for 3 minutes and add the watercress and coriander leaves. Stir again for a minute or so to get the noodles hotter.

❺ Put the noodles on a warmed serving platter, sprinkle the garnish of peanuts, dried shrimps and crushed chillies liberally over them and serve at once.

Rice paper rolls with a fresh crunchy filling

I first tasted these in a Vietnamese restaurant in Paris, and I've watched people enjoying them in the Vietnamese market in Melbourne. They were delicious, with their hot dipping sauce. I recall that the filling contained bits of bacon, omelette, plenty of mint and lettuce leaves. Here, I use mortadella rather than bacon and I don't cut up the omelette before I roll it inside the rice paper. **Serves 4 as a first course**

8 rice paper discs (the largest size)
4 thin slices of mortadella, the hard edges trimmed off and each slice cut in half
4 Cos lettuce leaves
handful of rocket
handful of Vietnamese mint or spearmint
handful of coriander leaves
2 small carrots, cut into tiny matchstick strips
2 measures of Nuoc Cham (page 31), divided among 4 small bowls, to serve

for the omelettes:
2 tablespoons clarified butter (page 140)
6 medium eggs, beaten
salt and freshly ground black pepper
1 teaspoon light soy sauce

1 First make the omelettes: heat 1 tablespoonful of the clarified butter in a non-stick frying pan, tilting the pan so that the butter covers the whole surface. Pour any excess back into the bowl of butter. Season the beaten egg with salt and pepper and the soy sauce. Pour a quarter of the egg into the pan and swirl it around to make a full round omelette. After 2 minutes, turn the omelette over and cook for 1 more minute. Transfer to a plate. Repeat this process to make 4 omelettes in total. Cut each in half to make 8 semi-circles.

2 Pour hot water into a large bowl. Dip one rice paper disc into this and leave it submerged for 30–45 seconds. Lift it out, lay it on a tray and pat it dry with kitchen paper.

3 To fill the rice paper roll: lay a semi-circle of mortadella on the side furthest from you. Then fill the nearer side with a semi-circle of omelette. Lay the lettuce leaves and rocket on this, followed by the mint, the coriander leaves and the tiny carrot matchstick strips. Start rolling the rice paper away from you. Make it a neat cigar shape, put it aside on an oval serving platter, and repeat the process until you have 8 filled rolls.

4 To serve: put 2 rolls on each of 4 plates and cut each roll across into 4 or 6 slices. Eat these with chopsticks, dipping each slice into your own bowl of Nuoc Cham.

Fried noodles with char-siu

Char-siu is the well-known Cantonese roast pork, available in the restaurants of any Chinatown. It is often displayed in the window, hanging from a hook next to the Peking duck. You can sometimes even buy it in large Chinese supermarkets.

Serves 4 as a main course

350–450 g / 12–16 oz bought char-siu (see above)
Basic Fried Noodles (page 51)
Cucumber Relish (page 47), to serve
Soy Sauce with Chilli (page 31), to serve

❶ Preheat the oven to 180°C/350°F/gas 4.
❷ Put the char-siu on a rack and heat it in the oven for 5–6 minutes.
❸ Meanwhile, prepare the Basic Fried Noodles (page 51). Cut the thoroughly heated-through char-siu into thick slices and lay these on top of the noodles.
❹ Serve hot, with Cucumber Relish (page 47) on the side and Soy Sauce with Chilli (page 31) as a dipping sauce.

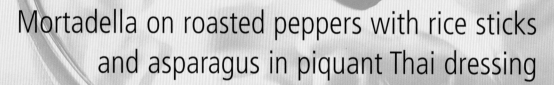

Mortadella on roasted peppers with rice sticks and asparagus in piquant Thai dressing

It is probably easier to roast your peppers a day in advance, and make sure you save the juice from the peppers so you can add it to the dressing. Allow one big round slice of mortadella per person. Serves 4 as a first course

4 peppers (2 red and 2 yellow)
olive oil for brushing
2 measures of Piquant Thai Dressing (page 35)
16 asparagus tips
salt

225 g / 8 oz rice sticks (narrow-ribbon kind), precooked as described on page 14
4 slices of mortadella, the hard edges trimmed off and each slice cut in half

1 Well ahead, ideally the day before, preheat the oven to 160°C/325°F/gas 3. Brush the peppers with olive oil, then roast them, still whole, for 30 minutes. Let them cool, then peel off their skins. Do this over a strainer, supported above a bowl, so that all the juice collects in the bowl. With a spoon, take out and discard the seeds from the peppers. Cut each pepper in half. Add the pepper juices to the Piquant Thai Dressing.

2 Shortly before you want to serve, put some of the piquant dressing in a bowl. Cook the asparagus tips in lightly salted boiling water for 4 minutes. Drain and put it in the piquant dressing.

3 When you are ready to serve, reheat the rice stick noodles and drain them well. Put them in a bowl and toss with 1 measure of the piquant dressing.

4 Divide the dressed noodles between 4 warmed plates, piling each portion on one side of the plate. Put half a red pepper on the other side of each plate, then half a yellow pepper slightly overlapping the red. Roll a half-slice of mortadella and place it on each pepper half. Arrange 2 asparagus tips likewise on each pepper half. Pour the remaining dressing over these and serve at room temperature.

NOODLE SALADS

Cellophane noodle salad with glazed prawns, jicama and apple

The English name for Mexican jicama, yam bean, suggests that the plant resembles any other kind of bean plant. It has pretty flowers, but they are toxic to humans and animals. The 'yam' is the tuber that grows in the soil. A native of tropical America, jicama is nowadays widely cultivated in India, China, Indonesia and East Africa. Easily found in any Chinatown, is it fruit or vegetable? For me it is a fruit; at least, I use it as one when I make rujak, a popular Indonesian hot-and-sweet fruit salad, but you can also treat it as a vegetable, eating it either raw or cooked. This combination of diced jicama, apples, noodles and prawns in a sweet, hot sauce is exotic and exciting, something not to be missed.
Serves 4 as a first course

1 jicama, peeled and diced
1–2 dessert apple(s) (Granny Smith or Cox's), peeled and diced
1 measure of Rujak Sauce (page 30)
2 small red chillies, deseeded and chopped
1 garlic clove, crushed
½ teaspoon salt
115 ml / 4 fl oz hot water
2 tablespoons chopped coriander leaves
2 teaspoons grated palm sugar (page 141) or soft brown sugar

2 teaspoons Thai fish sauce (*nam pla*, page 141)
24–32 peeled cooked king prawns
1 tablespoon lime juice
100 g / 3½ oz cellophane noodles, soaked in hot water for 5 minutes, drained, refreshed and drained again in a sieve, then cut into short lengths with scissors

1 As you prepare the jicama and apples, mix them into the Rujak Sauce so that they will not discolour. Set aside.

2 Put the chillies, garlic, salt and hot water in a wok or saucepan. Bring to the boil and bubble for 2 minutes. Add the coriander leaves, sugar and fish sauce. Stir these around over a moderate heat until the sugar has caramelized. Add the prawns, stir for 1 minute, add the lime juice and turn off the heat.

3 Put the noodles in a large bowl, add the prawn mixture and mix well.

4 To serve: put a portion of the jicama and apples on the side of each of 4 plates, pile the noodles and prawns on the other side and distribute the sauce around the edges. Serve warm or cold.

Cold soba noodles with lobster meat salad

If you prefer, you can use narrow-ribbon rice noodles here instead of soba. Whichever you choose, however, the noodles need to be mixed with half the dressing while they are still hot from their first cooking. This will help them to stay separate from each other when they are cold, and of course the flavours of the dressing will have time to penetrate. **Serves 2 as a main course or 4 as a first course**

salt
1 large whole uncooked or cooked lobster
225–350 g / 8–12 oz soba or rice-stick noodles
coriander leaves, to garnish
salad leaves, such as baby spinach, mizuna, rocket
and watercress, to dress (optional)

for the dressing:
3 tablespoons fish sauce (page 140)
2 tablespoons lime or lemon juice
2 tablespoons hot water
1–2 bird's-eye chillies, deseeded
  and chopped
4 spring onions, cut into thin rounds
handful of coriander leaves
1 teaspoon brown sugar
1 teaspoon finely chopped lemon grass
  (the inner part only)
1 teaspoon groundnut oil

1 In a large saucepan, boil about 1.75–2.25 litres (3–4 pints) of water with a large pinch of salt. When the water is boiling, plunge the whole lobster into it. Uncooked lobster needs to be boiled for 5 minutes; cooked lobster need be heated only for 1–2 minutes. Take the lobster out and let it cool.

2 While the lobster is cooking, make the dressing by mixing all the ingredients together.

3 At the same time, cook and drain the noodles as described on page 14, then immediately mix them in a bowl with half the dressing.

4 When the lobster is cool enough to handle, cut it in half lengthwise with a sharp knife. Discard the inedible parts (the head sac, gills and intestinal vein). Crush the claws and prise out the meat. Chop the body into fairly large pieces. Put them all into a bowl and mix with the remaining dressing.

5 To serve: divide the noodles among the appropriate number of plates and top each plate with a portion of dressed lobster. Add more coriander leaves to garnish, and some salad leaves if you wish. This noodle salad is to be eaten cold, but not chilled.

Cellophane noodle salad with prawns and smoked salmon

Whenever I go to Thailand I look forward to eating the spicy, fishy salads that are so popular there, many of them mixed with cellophane noodles for the contrast in flavour, texture and appearance. I love to make salads like this at home too, but I know that if I serve them at a dinner party the dressing will have too much chilli and fish sauce for some of my guests' tastes. This is a milder version, made entirely with ingredients that can be found anywhere, but by no means bland or lacking in bite. **Serves 8 as a good first course or 4 as a light lunch**

100 g / 3½ oz cellophane noodles
16 very small button mushrooms
salt and freshly ground black pepper
½ cucumber, cut in half
lengthwise and deseeded
16 large cooked king prawns
115 g / 4 oz smoked salmon,
cut into julienne strips
16 chicory leaves, to serve

for the dressing:
4 tablespoons lemon juice
2 teaspoons caster sugar
1 teaspoon salt
1 tablespoon light soy sauce
1 bird's-eye chilli, very finely chopped, or
a large pinch of cayenne pepper
1 small shallot, thinly sliced
1 tablespoon chopped spring onions
1 tablespoon chopped coriander leaves,
plus more whole sprigs to garnish

❶ Soak the cellophane noodles in hot water for 5–8 minutes. Drain and refresh under cold running water until cold, as described on page 14. Leave the noodles to drain in a sieve.

❷ Boil the mushrooms in salted water for 2 minutes. Drain, refresh in cold water and drain again.

❸ Slice the cucumber into half-moon shapes. Put these into a large glass bowl, then add all the ingredients for the dressing. Stir to dissolve the sugar and salt. This dressing can be prepared up to 4 hours in advance.

❹ When you are ready to serve the salad, cut up the noodles with scissors into 5–10-cm /2–4-inch lengths so that they will be easier to eat. Then mix the noodles, prawns, mushrooms and smoked salmon strips into the bowl of dressing and cucumber. Toss them well and serve on top of the chicory leaves.

Variation: With the same dressing and noodles, add 2 ripe avocados, each cut into 8 slices. In place of chicory, you can use 8 Cos lettuce leaves, and 200 g / 7 oz more smoked salmon, sliced, instead of prawns and mushrooms. The avocado, salmon and noodles on top of the lettuce leaves look particularly striking if you serve the dish on blue or yellow plates.

Nathan Fong's shrimp wonton salad

Once again, I have to thank my friend Nathan Fong in Vancouver for sharing his new recipe with me. Over there he uses what local people call rock shrimp; here in London I use raw king prawns. Serves 4 as a first course

24 round wonton wrappers
1 egg, lightly beaten
handful of coriander leaves, to garnish
handful of rocket leaves, to garnish

for the citrus soy vinaigrette:
4 tablespoons extra-virgin olive oil
2 teaspoons sesame oil
1 shallot, finely chopped
2 tablespoons Japanese brown rice vinegar
1 tablespoon light soy sauce
zest and juice of 1 lime
zest and juice of 1 lemon
freshly ground black pepper

for the filling:
225 g / 8 oz uncooked shelled king prawns, deveined and finely chopped
2 spring onions, cut into thin rounds
4 water chestnuts, finely chopped
2 tablespoons chopped coriander leaves
1 tablespoon sesame oil
¼ teaspoon chilli powder or freshly ground black pepper
1 garlic clove, finely chopped
zest and juice of 1 lemon
salt

❶ Mix all the ingredients for the filling thoroughly in a glass bowl. Fry a teaspoonful of it in a little oil and taste, then add more salt if necessary. Set aside in a cool place for 30 minutes.

❷ On a flat surface, place 2 rows of wonton wrappers, 3 in each row. Brush round their edges with beaten egg. Divide the filling into 12 portions, and put one portion on each of the 3 wrappers nearest you. Use the wrappers from the other row to cover these, and pinch round their edges to seal them well. Put these filled wonton ravioli on a tray lined with baking parchment (Bakewell paper) and fill the remaining wontons in the same way, so that you have 12 in all.

❸ Whisk together all the ingredients for the vinaigrette in a glass bowl and set aside.

❹ Bring a large pan of slightly salted water to a rolling boil. Cook the filled wontons in this, 6 at a time, for about 4 minutes each batch. When they are done, lift them out with a slotted spoon and drain on kitchen paper.

❺ To serve: arrange 3 cooked wontons on each of 4 plates, drizzle the vinaigrette all over them and garnish with coriander and rocket leaves. Serve at room temperature.

Piquant salad of cellophane vermicelli
wrapped in smoked salmon with cucumber and yoghurt

For the best presentation of this dish, you need ring moulds about
7.5 cm / 3 inches in diameter. Serves 4 as a first course or light lunch

30 g / 1 oz woodear fungus
100 g / 3½ oz cellophane vermicelli, soaked in hot
water for 5 minutes, then refreshed under
cold running water and drained well
1 measure Piquant Thai Dressing (page 35)
4 inner celery stalks, with the leaves, thickly sliced
5 tablespoons yoghurt
salt and freshly ground black pepper
1 thin cucumber, peeled and thinly sliced
4 large slices of smoked salmon, about
350–450 g / 12–16 oz total weight

❶ Soak the woodears in hot water for 5 minutes, then drain and slice them thinly.

❷ For this cold salad, the cellophane vermicelli need not be reheated. With scissors, chop it into short strands, roughly 5 cm / 2 inches in length. Put these in a bowl and toss them with the Thai dressing. Add the celery and woodears and mix everything well together.

❸ Whisk the yoghurt in a bowl with salt and pepper to taste. Add the cucumber slices and stir so that they are all well coated with the yoghurt.

❹ When you are ready to serve, put a ring mould (see above) in the centre of each of 4 plates, line each with a slice of salmon and pile cellophane vermicelli, woodears and celery inside, pressing them down a little with the back of a spoon. Lift the mould carefully away from its contents so as not to disturb the salmon. Spoon the cucumber and yoghurt around the salmon rings and serve immediately.

Vietnamese rice paper rolls with herb salad

In my recent travels I've eaten these rice-paper rolls, in one form or another and with various fillings, on the US West Coast and in Australia and Singapore. I admit that I have not encountered them in Britain, though I'm fairly certain they are to be found here. They are sure of a welcome, provided they are freshly made and served immediately. **Makes 4 rolls (serves 4 people as a first course)**

1 litre / 1¾ pints hot (not boiling) water
8 circular sheets of rice paper, 28 cm /
11 inches in diameter
8 young Cos lettuce leaves, coarsely shredded
30 g / 1 oz rice vermicelli, precooked
as described on page 14
115 g / 4 oz cooked honey-roast ham,
cut into julienne strips
16 peeled cooked king prawns
2 hard-boiled eggs, sliced
2 tablespoons roughly chopped mint
2 tablespoons roughly chopped coriander leaves

for the dressing:
2 teaspoons Dijon mustard
juice of 2 limes
2 teaspoons chopped chives
1 tablespoon white wine vinegar
1 teaspoon sugar (optional)
115 ml / 4 fl oz extra-virgin olive oil
salt and freshly ground black pepper

for the salad:
225 g / 8 oz rocket leaves
handful of coriander leaves
handful of mint leaves

❶ Make the dressing: in a glass bowl, mix the mustard with the lime juice. Add the chives, vinegar and sugar, whisking with a fork. Then add the olive oil, a little at a time, still whisking. Add the last of the olive oil in a continuous stream, whisking continually until the dressing becomes fairly thick. Season to taste with salt and pepper.

❷ To fill the rolls: put the hot water into a bowl. Take 2 rice paper discs and dip them into the water one at a time, leaving each immersed for 15 seconds to allow it to soften. Lay the first disc on a flat surface, pat dry with kitchen paper, then lay the second on top of it and pat that dry also. Spread a quarter of the shredded lettuce across this double-thickness disk, leaving about 1 cm / ½ inch clear around the edge. Sprinkle the lettuce with 1 teaspoonful of the dressing. Next arrange a quarter of the noodles on top of the lettuce, then a quarter each of the ham, prawns, egg, mint and coriander. Finish with another teaspoonful of dressing over the whole pile. Fold the left and right sides of the rice-paper disks inwards, then roll up the rice paper, starting from the edge nearest you, so that all the filling is firmly rolled and held inside. Repeat to make 4 rolls in all.

❸ When you are ready to serve, dress the salad ingredients with the remaining dressing and divide between 4 plates. Cut each roll into 3 slices and arrange these on top of the salad. Serve and eat at once.

Green papaya and mango salad with cellophane noodles and marinated salmon and sea bass

This is a Southeast Asian raw fish salad – though not truly raw, as the juices of the papaya, mango and lime (or lemon) do actually cook the fish very slightly. Make sure that you buy the freshest of fish. Serves 4 as a first course

1 small green papaya, peeled, deseeded and the flesh either grated or cut into tiny matchstick strips
1 tablespoon salt
1 slightly unripe mango, peeled and sliced into tiny matchstick strips
115 g / 4 oz cellophane noodles, soaked in hot water for 5 minutes, refreshed under cold running water, then drained and cut into short lengths with scissors
1 measure of Piquant Thai Dressing (page 35)

225 g / 8 oz skinless salmon fillet, cut into thin slices
225 g / 8 oz skinless sea bass fillet, cut into thin slices
juice of 2 limes or lemons
½ teaspoon fine sea salt
4 Cos lettuce leaves, to serve
1–2 large red chillies, deseeded and sliced, to garnish

❶ Put the papaya flesh in a bowl and mix in the tablespoonful of salt. Leave for 30 minutes. Then wash the papaya in a sieve to rinse away the salt. Drain and transfer to a large bowl.

❷ Add the mango and noodles to the bowl and pour over the dressing. Toss and mix well.

❸ Put the slices of fish in another bowl. Add the lime or lemon juice and the fine sea salt. Mix well, leave to stand for 2–4 minutes, then mix in with the noodle mixture and leave to stand for 2 more minutes.

❹ To serve: put a Cos lettuce leaf on each of 4 large plates. Divide the noodle salad equally between the lettuce leaves; if the leaves are not big enough to contain whole portions, let some fall on the plates. Serve cold, garnished with slices of red chilli.

Salad of cold somen with avocado dipping sauce and stuffed chicken rolls

My reason for including in the first part of this book as many recipes for dipping sauces as space allowed is that each sauce can be used with many different recipes. So do read those early pages as a guide to creating variations on recipes, and to adapting sauces to different uses – also to making basic sauces in large quantities for cold storage, so that you always have them ready for use at short notice. **Serves 4 as a lunch or supper or 8 as a first course**

175–225 g / 6–8 oz somen noodles, cooked as described on page 14 and drained well
Spicy Avocado Dipping Sauce (page 30, made with 2 avocados)
handful (or more) of watercress or rocket

for the chicken rolls:
3–4 skinless chicken breast fillets (about 450 g / 1 lb in total), diced
2 eggs, lightly beaten
1 teaspoon very finely chopped root ginger
½ teaspoon salt
1 garlic clove, crushed
2 teaspoons cornflour, dissolved in 2 tablespoons cold water
1 tablespoon light soy sauce
1 teaspoon sugar

for the stuffing:
salt and freshly ground black pepper
2 small carrots, diced
1 parsnip, diced
2 tablespoons clarified butter
4 chestnut mushrooms, stalks removed and heads cut into small dice
4 tablespoons chopped coriander or parsley
1 tablespoon light soy sauce

❶ Put all ingredients for the chicken rolls in a blender or food processor and blend until smooth. Transfer to a plate and keep in a cool place.

❷ Prepare the stuffing: in separate small pans of lightly salted boiling water, blanch the carrots and parsnips for 2 minutes and 1 minute respectively. Drain, refresh in cold water and drain well again.

❸ Heat the clarified butter in a non-stick frying pan and stir-fry the mushrooms for 2 minutes. Add the coriander or parsley and stir for a minute, then stir in the carrots and parsnips. Season with ½ teaspoon each salt and pepper, and the soy sauce. Continue stir-frying for just 1 more minute, then turn off the heat and let cool.

❹ Divide the chicken mixture into 3. Lay a piece of cling-film on a tray and put one portion of the minced chicken on the cling-film, moulding and pressing it to form a square, as if you were making pastry. Spread

one-third of the stuffing in a strip across the middle of the square. Now pick up the edge of cling-film nearest you and carefully roll up the stuffing inside the chicken to make a kind of sausage. (Take care not to get the edge of the cling-film into the sausage.) At the two ends, twist the cling-film to seal it and tie it with string. Repeat this process so that you have 3 rolls.

5 Lay the rolls on a plate that will fit into a steamer and steam them for 10–15 minutes. Let them cool a little, unwrap them from the cling-film and cut each roll across into slices about 1 cm / ½ inch thick.

6 To serve: arrange the noodles on 4 or 8 plates. Spoon equal portions of the dipping sauce over the noodles. Arrange the sliced chicken rolls around each pile of noodles. Top with watercress or rocket, or toss everything together in a bowl. Serve at room temperature.

Warm salad of duck, French beans and roasted peppers with fried rice-stick noodles

As a rule, when I am cooking just for two I don't want to spend more than 20 minutes in the kitchen before I sit down to enjoy the food. This is one of the recipes that I make often. Remember, though, to roast the peppers well beforehand – on the previous day, even – because this takes 30 minutes.

Serves 2 as a one-bowl meal or 4 as a first course

2 peppers (preferably 1 red and 1 yellow)
225 g / 8 oz French beans
3 tablespoons olive oil
2 skinless duck breast fillets, cut into thin julienne strips
½ teaspoon salt
¼ teaspoon freshly ground black pepper
6 anchovies, drained and chopped
1 tablespoon white wine vinegar
2 teaspoons sugar
1 teaspoon lemon juice

for the fried noodles:
2 tablespoons sunflower oil
4 shallots, chopped
2 garlic cloves, chopped
about ½ teaspoon chilli powder
1 teaspoon chopped root ginger
3 slices of bacon, chopped
4 tablespoons chopped parsley
2 tablespoons light soy sauce
3 ripe tomatoes, skinned and chopped
175–225 g / 6–8 oz rice-stick noodles (the wide-ribbon kind), precooked as described on page 14

❶ Prepare the salad vegetables: roast the peppers as described on page 121 for 30–35 minutes and, when cool enough to handle, peel and cut into strips. Strain the juice from the peppers, discarding seeds. Blanch the beans in lightly salted water for 4 minutes, drain and refresh in cold water. Drain again and pat dry.
❷ Cook the fried noodles: heat the oil in a wok and stir-fry the shallots, garlic, chilli, ginger and bacon for 5 minutes. Add the parsley and soy sauce, and stir-fry for 2 more minutes. Add the tomatoes and stir-fry for another 2 minutes. Add the noodles and stir until well mixed. Adjust the seasoning, then turn off the heat.
❸ To cook the duck: heat the oil in a frying pan and fry the duck strips, stirring frequently, over a high heat for 2 minutes. Lower the heat, add the salt and stir-fry for 2–3 minutes more. Add the black pepper, anchovies, roasted peppers with their juices and the beans. Stir, cover and leave over a moderate heat for 1–2 minutes. Uncover and stir again for 1 minute. Taste and add the vinegar, sugar, lemon juice and more salt if necessary.
❹ Serve the duck warm on top of the fried noodles, accompanied by a green salad.

Rice noodle salad with spiced minced duck breast

This can also be made with cellophane noodles and served cold or warm as a first course, or as a light lunch accompanied by a green salad. **Serves 4 as a one-bowl meal or 8 as a first course**

2 tablespoons groundnut oil
3 shallots, finely chopped
2–4 bird's-eye chillies, finely chopped
4–6 skinless duck breast fillets, minced
6-cm / 2½-inch piece of lemon grass stalk, the outer leaves discarded and the soft inner part finely chopped
4 tablespoons chicken stock
3 tablespoons lemon juice

2 tablespoons Thai fish sauce (*nam pla*, see page 141)
2 kaffir lime leaves (page 141), thinly sliced (optional)
225 g / 8 oz noodles, precooked as described on page 14
2 tablespoons finely chopped spring onions
salt and freshly ground black pepper
handful of coriander leaves, to garnish

❶ Heat the oil in a wok or frying pan and stir-fry the shallots and chillies for 2 minutes. Add the minced duck breast and stir-fry for 2 more minutes. Add the remaining ingredients, except the noodles, spring onions and coriander. Increase the heat and continue cooking over a high heat until all liquid has been absorbed. Add the spring onions and adjust the seasoning.

❷ Reheat the noodles as described on page 16, drain well and put in a large serving bowl. Add the duck mixture and toss to mix everything well together. Serve immediately.

Soba noodles with peking duck salad

Order whole Peking duck in a Chinese restaurant and the crisp skin will be cut up and served as a first course, wrapped in pancakes smeared with Hoisin sauce and accompanied by julienned spring onions and cucumber. The meat is stir-fried and served as the main course, with fried rice or noodles. A duck prepared in this way makes an excellent one-dish meal at home. Reserve wings and carcass for stock and use the legs in Vietnamese Noodle Soup with Steamed Duck (page 97). Frozen cooked Peking duck is available from Chinese supermarkets and, increasingly, from better high-street supermarkets. **Serves 4–6 as first course or 2–3 as a light lunch**

1 ready-cooked Peking duck (from an old-style Chinese restaurant, where the ducks are hung in the window) or 1 frozen cooked Peking duck
350–450 g / 12–16 oz dried soba noodles, cooked and drained as described on page 14

1 tablespoon light soy sauce
2–3 tablespoons Hoisin sauce
8 spring onions, sliced thinly at an angle
½ cucumber, peeled, deseeded and cut into short sticks
½ teaspoon cayenne pepper (optional)

1 If using frozen duck, allow it to thaw completely, then roast it in an oven preheated to 180°C/350°F/gas 4 for 45 minutes, starting with the breast upwards, turning it over after 15 minutes, and turning it breast-up again after a further 15 minutes. Leave it to cool a little, then continue as described in step 3, below.

2 If using ready-cooked duck from a restaurant kitchen, roast it as above for 30 minutes only, starting with the breast upwards, and turning it over after 15 minutes. Leave it to cool a little, then continue as follows.

3 Cut off wings and legs. Reserve the legs for noodle soup and the wings for the stockpot (with the carcass, later). Separate meat and crisp skin. Slice the meat and cut the skin into julienne strips with a very sharp knife.

4 Reheat the noodles as described on page 16, drain and toss with half of each of the sauces. Arrange them attractively at the sides of each of 4 plates and stack slices of duck on top. Pile the cucumber and spring onions on the other sides and dribble around the remaining sauces. Sprinkle with cayenne pepper if you like.

Glossary of more unusual ingredients

ANCHOVIES, DRIED Very small dried anchovies (or possibly whitebait) are sold in packets in Oriental food shops. They may be labelled *ikan bilis* or *ikan teri*. Buy the ones without heads if you can; if the heads are still on, it is better to remove them.

BAMBOO SHOOTS Don't bother looking for fresh ones. Canned ones (or the baby ones in glass jars) are as good, and far less trouble. Once the can or jar has been opened, unused shoots will keep for up to 10 days in the fridge, if they are stored in water that is changed daily.

BEANCURD, see tofu

BEANSPROUTS These can now be bought almost everywhere, but make sure you get fresh, crisp ones. For appearance's sake, it is worth spending time going through the packet, breaking off and discarding the brownish roots.

BIRD'S-EYE CHILLI, see chilli

BONITO FLAKES, see *katsuobushi*

CANDLENUTS These are available from many Oriental shops, sometimes labelled *kemiri*. Don't eat them uncooked as they are mildly toxic. Macadamia nuts are a good substitute, and if even these are not to hand almonds will do.

CHAR SIU Cantonese roasted pork, it can be bought, ready to eat, from many Cantonese restaurants, and in the more traditional ones you will see large pieces of *char siu* hanging from a rack, usually next to some Peking ducks; both have the same rather glossy dark-brown surface.

CHILLI, BIRD'S-EYE The general rule with chillies is that the smallest are the hottest. Bird's-eye chillies (also called bird chillies) are very small, and either bright red or bright green. Colour doesn't affect flavour or hotness. Capsaicin, the 'hot' constituent of chillies, though completely harmless, can cause discomfort to sensitive areas of skin, the eyes, sometimes even fingers, as well as the tongue, so wash your hands after handling chillies. If you get a mouthful of unbearable hotness, cold rice or cool cucumber is soothing;

iced water and cold beer are little help. Alcohol can dissolve capsaicin, but you need plenty of it – neat whisky is said to be effective.

CHILLI OIL Giving a mild tang of chilli to whatever it's cooked with, versions of this flavoured oil are widely available. Commercially produced oil is actually crushed from fresh chilli seeds, but you can make your own by slicing 4 or 5 dried red chillies very finely and letting them steep for at least a week in about 100–150 ml / 4–6 fl oz of oil – any good-quality oil will do, but extra-virgin olive oil is, of course, the best.

CLARIFIED BUTTER This is much the same as Indian ghee, though ghee has more flavour. To clarify butter (i.e. get rid of the solids – sugars and milk protein – it contains), heat it gently until there is no more froth. The solids are deposited on the bottom of the pan. Strain the liquid butter through fine muslin.

COCONUT MILK This is not the water that, in the tropics, you drink from freshly cut young green nuts. It is a white liquid obtained from the flesh of a mature nut, somewhat rich in saturated fats but with no cholesterol. It is almost universally used as a cooking medium in coconut-growing countries. I have described, in other books, how to make this *santan* from fresh coconut meat or desiccated coconut flakes, but I rarely do this myself nowadays since there are several reliable brands of canned coconut milk on sale in Oriental food stores, which give results that are almost indistinguishable from fresh *santan*.

DRIED ANCHOVIES, see anchovies

DRIED SHRIMP, see shrimp, dried

FISH SAUCE Often called in the West by its Thai name, *nam pla*, or Vietnamese *nuoc mam*, this is more or less a liquid version of shrimp paste (q.v.): a salty, tangy concoction considered essential for savoury dishes in many parts of Southeast Asia. It can easily be bought in any Oriental food shop in the West, usually in 75-cl bottles. My favourite brand is called Squid and

has a picture of a squid on the label, but this is only a trademark; as far as I know the sauce doesn't contain any squid.

GALANGAL (OR GALINGALE) This is a rhizome, like ginger, though it is pinker and more delicate-looking, and the flavour is quite different – more sour than hot. The Thai name for it is *ka*. It is fairly easy to find in Oriental shops, either fresh or dried and ground. Fresh galangal should be peeled and chopped, like ginger.

GINGER JUICE If you aren't all that fond of the taste of chopped ginger, you can use ginger juice to achieve much the same aromatic effect in a dish. To make this, grate some fresh ginger, leave it for a few minutes in a teaspoonful or two of tepid water, then squeeze the gratings in a garlic crusher and press them through a fine-mesh sieve.

HOISIN SAUCE This Cantonese condiment, used as a marinade and as a sauce for Peking duck, is easily obtainable in Chinese shops and many Western supermarkets. Its fruity, almost plummy flavour gives little clue to its ingredients, which are largely rice, wheat, soy beans and sugar.

KAFFIR LIME LEAF These shiny dark-green leaves can be bought, in small packets, in most Thai and other Oriental food shops. They impart a mildly bitter, citrusy taste to dishes they are cooked with. In some recipes, they are shredded and can be eaten. When left whole, they should be discarded before serving.

KATSUOBUSHI These are shavings of dried bonito fillet, essential for Japanese cooking. The fish is boiled, dried, smoked, and finally cured with a mould similar to the mould used in making soy sauce. *Katsuobushi* can be bought in many Oriental shops; it is expensive, but you need to use only a little at a time.

KELP, see *konbu*

KONBU This is the Japanese name for kelp, a broad, flat-leafed species of seaweed used extensively in Japanese kitchens. Like other Japanese ingredients, it is not difficult to find in the West but it is expensive. It is absolutely necessary as the basic flavour of dashi stock (see page 21).

LEMON GRASS Lemon grass hardly needs any introduction as nowadays it is on sale almost everywhere. Most recipes in this book require the tough outer layer(s) of the stem to be stripped off and discarded. The soft inner part, though rather fibrous, is easily sliced into thin rounds. When cooked as part of a dressing or sauce, it looks attractive and has a pleasantly, slightly lemony flavour.

MIRIN A popular flavouring in Japan, made of fermented steamed glutinous rice mixed with distilled alcohol and matured for between 1 and 2 months. This gives it a sweet taste, which it contributes to dishes cooked with it.

MISO This staple of Japanese cookery is a paste of soy beans, rice or barley and salt fermented with an *Aspergillus* mould. The result is very nutritious, rich in protein and highly flavoured. There are several kinds of miso, but those you will most often find in the West are white miso (made from soy beans and rice) and red miso (soy beans and barley). Miso is sold in sealed plastic packets, but even when opened it will keep in the fridge for at least a month.

NAM PLA, see fish sauce

NUOC MAM, see fish sauce

ONIONS, CRISP-FRIED It is easy enough to make your own (page 44), but many shops sell plastic tubs of factory-made fried onions which are just as good. They may also be labelled 'fried shallots'.

PALM SUGAR This is crystallized from the sweet juice of the flower of the coconut palm, and should be dark red in colour. It is sold in hard blocks and sometimes appears in the West under its old name of *jaggery*. To use it, you will need either to grate the block with a coarse grater, or knock a chunk off with a hammer. Then put it in boiling water and stir until it dissolves – this can take several minutes.

SAKE The celebrated Japanese rice wine is in fact brewed, not vinified; but to call it rice beer would

give quite the wrong impression of this refined drink, the alcohol level of which is roughly that of sherry. Any good average sake that has got as far as the export market is adequate for cooking.

SESAME, OIL; SEED; PASTE I use sesame oil as an ingredient for dressings etc. because of its characteristic and quite strong flavour; I never use it for frying, where the flavour would interfere with the food. Instructions for making sesame seed paste are on page 36, but I usually buy the paste ready-made.

SHAOHSING WINE This Chinese rice wine is used almost exclusively for cooking. Widely available in Oriental stores, it is very easy to identify as it comes in bottles shaped like smaller whisky bottles.

SHOYU, see soy sauce

SHRIMP, DRIED Also sometimes labelled dried prawns, these are sold in Asian shops in packets, already shelled, salted and roasted. Their flavour is strong, so use them sparingly. In most recipes they need to be soaked in hot water for 5–10 minutes before use.

SHRIMP PASTE This is a very pungent condiment beloved of Southeast Asian cooks and I cannot imagine cooking without it. You can buy it, in square 250-g or 8-oz blocks, in most Oriental food stores, often under the names *terasi* (Indonesian), *blachen* or *balachan* (Malaysian), or *kapi* (Thai). The paste will keep indefinitely, outside the fridge, but once the packet is opened it should be stored in an airtight container, otherwise the smell will spread through your house.

In cooking, use only very small quantities: about 5 g / under ¼ oz is ample for a dish for 4–6 people. If a recipe calls for the shrimp paste to be roasted, cut a slice from the block about 5 mm / ¼ inch thick, wrap it loosely in aluminium foil, and bake it in a low oven for 5 minutes. Better still, cut the block into slices, spread them in one layer and wrap them in a double thickness of foil, then bake all of them at one go and store them in a glass jar until needed.

You can sometimes buy pre-sliced, ready-roasted shrimp paste, but supplies seem to be very intermittent and it is better to roast your own. A slice of shrimp paste can also be grilled or dry-fried in a non-stick frying pan (without any foil). The smell is strong, but not unpleasant.

SICHUAN (OR SZECHUAN) PEPPER Sichuan peppercorns, which come from the prickly ash tree, look and taste quite different from the black and white peppercorns people are accustomed to in the West. They are now widely available and are essential if you want the real Sichuan flavour, which is usually released by crushing and gently heating the seeds. Also known as anise pepper, fagara or sansho pepper, it is an essential element in Chinese five-spice powder.

SOY SAUCE, DARK; LIGHT; SHOYU; TAMARI The soya bean is a wonderful vegetable, full of proteins – and, luckily for Asia, these proteins complement the ones found in rice and make up the full list that the human body requires, so, in theory, soya bean eaters don't need meat. Unfortunately, much of the bean's nutritional value lies in parts of it that the human body cannot digest. The solution is to ferment the beans with moulds that can break down these parts and make them available to us when we eat them. This is one reason why Asian cuisines seem to have an obsession with fermented soya bean products, though their inventors presumably knew little or nothing about the biochemistry involved – they simply liked the taste.

Among such products is the whole range of soy sauces, tangy and savoury, with varying levels of saltiness and sweetness. For the recipes in this book, the important contrast is between light soy, which is salty and rather thin, and dark soy, which is somewhat sweeter and somewhat thicker and more treacly – though it still pours easily. My preferred brand of light soy is made in China and sold in virtually all Oriental shops in Britain. The same firm does a very good dark soy.

The Japanese produce a wide range, but the most easily available is Kikkoman, which you will find in almost any food shop and supermarket.

I would class this a moderately dark soy. Dutch-made Indonesian-style sauces, usually labelled *kecap manis* ('*kecap*' is where the English word ketchup comes from; '*manis*' is 'sweet') are thick, heavy and too sweet for my taste.

Shoyu is simply the Japanese word for soy sauce, but the word is understood, in the West, to mean a particular kind of soy that can usually be found only in Japanese food shops and large Chinese stores. Its flavour is richer and saltier than Kikkoman, and needless to say it costs more. It is worth the extra money, but if you cannot get it then Kikkoman, or failing that any other good-quality soy sauce, will do quite well.

Tamari is a rather superior and expensive kind of soy sauce made without wheat; it goes particularly well with *sashimi*. This, as far as I have observed, is only obtainable in the West in specialist Japanese shops.

TAHINA This sesame seed paste from the eastern Mediterranean is very similar to that sold in Chinese and other Oriental shops and supermarkets.

TAMARI, see soy sauce

TAMARIND WATER The fruit of the tamarind tree has been popular for many centuries for the pleasantly sour flavour it gives to cooked food. You can buy fresh tamarind in Britain, with the flesh and seeds still enclosed in brittle, lumpy pods; but it is more often sold in plastic-wrapped blocks, minus the shells but with flesh and seeds pressed together into a compact mass. In this book, tamarind is used in the form of tamarind water.

To make a cup of tamarind water (about 220 ml / 8 fl oz) you need about 40 g / up to 1½ oz of tamarind flesh, broken or cut from the block, or the contents of two tamarind pods. Put the flesh in a bowl and pour over it a cupful of warm water. Then press and squeeze the flesh, with your fingers or a spoon, to get the juice out of it and make the water a rich brown colour. When you think you've got as much as you can, strain everything through a sieve and discard the seeds and scraps of flesh. If you make a larger quantity

of tamarind water, you can store it as ice cubes; it will keep in the freezer for up to 3 months.

Alternatively, put 450 g / 1 lb of tamarind flesh into a pan with 1.1 litres / 2 pints of water. Bring the water to the boil and simmer until the water has reduced to half its volume. Strain this, discard the solids and simmer the water again for 10 minutes. Then leave the liquid to get cold. This tamarind water will be about twice as thick and strong-tasting as the kind described above, so you should dilute it with equal parts of water before use, unless you prefer the stronger flavour.

TOFU, COTTON; FRIED; SILKEN As the English name beancurd suggests, this is made from a 'milk' extracted from soya beans and then curdled to make a more or less solid block, with the texture and appearance of junket. It is rich in proteins but has little flavour of its own. However, it picks up and absorbs flavours from the sauces with which it is cooked.

Fresh Chinese-style tofu is available in blocks, weighing about 450 g / 1 lb, in all Chinese shops and some Thai shops. Japanese shops, if they sell these, usually call them 'Shanghai tofu'. Chinese tofu will keep, if submerged in water with the water changed daily, for up to 4 days in the fridge.

Japanese 'cotton' and 'silken' tofu will keep for a long time as long as the packets remain unopened; once open, they should be used within a few days. 'Cotton' is firm enough to slice; 'silken' is very soft.

Fried tofu consists of chunks of fresh tofu that have been deep-fried to give them a slightly chewy but absorbent skin. This adds a more interesting texture to the tofu and helps it to take up the flavours of ingredients with which it is cooked. You can fry your own, but it's much more convenient to buy it ready-made from a Chinese shop.

VIETNAMESE MINT (RAU RAM) This is not really mint at all, simply another name for one of the two kinds of Thai basil – the kind that has long, pointed green leaves with purple markings. In a Thai shop, if you ask for Thai basil you are more likely to get the right plant. In the recipes in this book, I suggest spearmint as a substitute.

VINEGAR, BROWN RICE; WHITE WINE Any Japanese cook will tell you that 'real' brown rice vinegar is virtually unobtainable outside Japan, and very expensive there. However, exported branded brown rice vinegars, such as Mitsukan, are widely available and satisfactory for cooking. White wine vinegar can be found in any supermarket.

WOODEARS (OFTEN LABELLED 'BLACK FUNGUS') These represent one of several types of Chinese dried mushroom (cloudears are another). They are easy enough to find, though expensive to buy. However, a small quantity goes a long way. They are valued for their texture as much as for their flavour.

YELLOW BEAN SAUCE Yellow (and black) beans, in various forms, can be bought from most Oriental shops. All are variations on salted, fermented soya beans, and they are indeed very salty. Black beans are used when the cook wants the dish to be dark-coloured; yellow beans make the sauce just nicely golden.

YOGHURT For the recipes in this book, I would choose Greek-style yoghurt, but any natural, unflavoured runny yoghurt should be satisfactory.

Acknowledgements and Bibliography

I have been learning about noodles practically all my life, so I have many more people to thank than I can name here. I can only list some of those who have helped me, and often given me hospitality as well, during my recent research for this book. Whether you are named or not, please accept my grateful thanks.

In London: Lewis Esson, Mary Evans, Sarah Emery, Gus Filgate and Will Heap, Anne Furniss, Richard Hosking, Deh-Ta Hsiung, Jane Suthering and Olivier Laudus.

In Vancouver: Nathan Fong and, in Vancouver Island, Sinclair Philip.

In Singapore: at the Four Seasons Hotel, Neil Jacobs, Sam Leong and Joachin Tan.

As always, my thanks go also to my husband, Roger, and my agent, John McLaughlin, for helping to make the path to publication smoother.

Finally, I acknowledge my debt to the authors of the following books, which I have consulted during my work on noodles:

K.C. Chang (ed.): *Food in Chinese Culture* (Yale, 1977)

Alan Davidson: *The Oxford Companion to Food* (OUP, 1999)

Lesley Downer: *At the Japanese Table* (Chronicle Books, 1993)

Richard Hosking: *The Dictionary of Japanese Food* (Charles Tuttle, 1996; Prospect Books)

Deh-Ta Hsiung: *The Chinese Kitchen* (Kyle Cathie, 1999)

Harold McGee: *On Food and Cooking* (Allen & Unwin, 1984)

Anne Willan: *Complete Guide to Cookery* (Dorling Kindersley, 1989)

First published in 2000 by
Quadrille Publishing Limited,
Alhambra House,
27–31 Charing Cross Road,
London WC2H OLS

Cataloguing-in-Publication Data: a catalogue record for this book is available from the British Library.

ISBN 1 902757 47 5

Publishing Director: Anne Furniss
Art Director: Mary Evans
Editor & Project Manager: Lewis Esson
Design Assistant: Sarah Emery
Food for Photography: Jane Suthering assisted by Olivier Laudus
Styling: Penny Markham
Production: Julie Hadingham

Printed and bound in Hong Kong by Dai Nippon

Colour separations by Colourscan, Singapore

Index

anchovies, crisp-fried dried, 43
Asian stock, 23
asparagus tips in clear broth, 70-1
aubergines: caramelized shallots
  and, 59
  noodles with roasted tomatoes
  and, 49
avocados: avocado and tofu
  tempura in miso soup, 64
  avocado dipping sauce, 30

beef: beef stock, 25
  black-peppered beef, 109
  noodle soup with lemon grass
  and, 105
  noodles with chilli beef, 111
  udon soup with sautéed beef
  and bamboo shoots, 106
beetroot and anchovy dipping
  sauce, 27
Burmese fish soup, 81

cabbage, crisp-fried green, 43
cellophane noodles, 10, 14
  salads, 123, 127
chicken: basic chicken stock, 24
  casserole of noodles with
  hot-marinated fried chicken, 93
  chicken dumpling soup, 88
  chicken wing party noodles, 91
  chicken wontons with blushed
  tomatoes, 94
  egg noodles with shiitake
  mushrooms and, 90
  Indonesian chicken soup, 87
  salad of cold somen with stuffed
  chicken rolls, 134-5
chilli sauce, 33
chow mein, Sichuan prawn, 79
coconut dressing, 37
cod: caramelized cod fillet on rice
  vermicelli, 82

condiments, 42-7
cucumber relish, 47
curry pastes, 38-41

dashi, 21
dipping sauces, 26-33
dressings, 34-7
duck: Balinese satays, 100
  braised duck on seaweed, 96
  rice noodle salad with spiced
  minced duck breast, 137
  Sam Leong's Shanghainese
  noodles, 98-9
  soba noodles with Peking duck
  salad, 139
  Vietnamese noodle soup with
  steamed duck, 97
  warm salad of duck, French beans
  and roasted peppers, 136

egg noodles, 9, 14

fish stock, 21

green curry paste, 40

Japanese dipping sauce, 28

laksa, 72-5
  paste for, 41
lamb: parsleyed egg noodles with
  lamb kofta in red curry sauce, 112
  rack of lamb with asparagus
  noodles, 108
lobster meat salad: cold soba
  noodles with, 124

miso stock, 23
monkfish, tea-smoked, 84-5
mortadella on roasted peppers,
  120-1
mushrooms: fried noodles on
  Portobello mushrooms, 53

Nathan Fong's shrimp wonton
  salad, 128
noodles: basic fried noodles, 51
  crisp-fried noodles, 44
nuoc cham, 31

pad thai, 117
peanuts, garlic-flavoured fried, 45
piquant dressings, 35
pork: barbecued spare ribs with
  shiitake noodles, 114-15
  fried noodles with char-siu, 119
  pad thai, 117
prawns: cellophane noodle salad
  with glazed prawns, jicama and
  apple, 123
  cellophane noodle salad with
  smoked salmon and, 127
  chopped prawn and quails' egg
  wonton soup, 69
  Nathan Fong's shrimp wonton
  salad, 128
  Sichuan prawn chow mein, 79

quail stuffed with noodles, 103

red curry paste, 39
relish, cucumber, 47
rice noodles, 10, 14
rice papers, 13
  rice paper rolls with a fresh
  crunchy filling, 118
root vegetables with egg noodles,
  55
Rujak sauce, 30

salads, 122-39
salmon, green papaya and mango
  salad with, 132
Sam Leong's Shanghainese
  noodles, 98-9
sauces, 26-33

scallops: laksa with udon, quails'
  eggs and, 73
  pan-fried scallops with chicory
  and apples, 77
seafood: laksa with hot seafood
  pot, 74
'seaweed', 43
shallots, crisp-fried, 44
Singapore fried noodles, 80
smoked salmon, piquant salad of
  cellophane vermicelli wrapped
  in, 129
soba noodles, 11, 14, 19
  soba noodle soup with shiitake
  mushrooms, 63
somen noodles, 11, 14
soups, 63-4, 69-75, 81, 87-9, 97,
  105-6
soy sauce with chilli, 31
spinach, timbale of fried noodles
  and, 54
spring rolls, 13, 66-7
squid, Vietnamese stuffed, 78
stocks, 20-5

Thai dressing, 35
tofu: coconut, tofu and pumpkin
  noodles, 65
  fine egg noodles with scrambled
  tofu, 50
  layered rice sticks with, 56-7
  tofu dressing, 36
tomatoes, blushed, 47

udon noodles, 11, 14
  vegetarian udon casserole, 60

Vietnamese rice paper rolls, 130-1

wheat flour egg noodles, 18
wonton skins, 13
wrappers, 13